my re

OCR

RE...AND DIS...NDER THE TUDORS
1485–1603

Nicholas Fellows

HODDER
EDUCATION
AN HACHETTE UK COMPANY

Acknowledgements

The Publishers would like to thank the following for permission to reproduce copyright material.

pp.75 *A*, **80** *B* **& 83** *A* C. Haigh, *English Reformations: Religion, Politics and Society under the Tudors*, 1993. Used by permission of The Oxford University Press; **pp.75** *B*, **77** *A* **& 80** *A* Edward Arnold Publishers Ltd; **pp.83** *B*, **85** *B* **& 88** *A* Reprinted by permission of The Kent State University Press. From *Rebellion and Riot* (1982, The Kent State Univ. Press) by Barrett L. Beer.

Every effort has been made to trace all copyright holders, but if any have been inadvertently overlooked, the Publishers will be pleased to make the necessary arrangements at the first opportunity.

Although every effort has been made to ensure that website addresses are correct at time of going to press, Hodder Education cannot be held responsible for the content of any website mentioned in this book. It is sometimes possible to find a relocated web page by typing in the address of the home page for a website in the URL window of your browser.

Hachette UK's policy is to use papers that are natural, renewable and recyclable products and made from wood grown in sustainable forests. The logging and manufacturing processes are expected to conform to the environmental regulations of the country of origin.

Orders: please contact Bookpoint Ltd, 130 Milton Park, Abingdon, Oxon OX14 4SE. Telephone: +44 (0)1235 827720. Fax: +44 (0)1235 400401. Email education@bookpoint.co.uk Lines are open from 9 a.m. to 5 p.m., Monday to Saturday, with a 24-hour message answering service. You can also order through our website: www.hoddereducation.co.uk

ISBN: 978 1 5104 1643 7

© Nicholas Fellows 2018

First published in 2018 by
Hodder Education,
An Hachette UK Company
Carmelite House
50 Victoria Embankment
London EC4Y 0DZ

www.hoddereducation.co.uk

Impression number   10 9 8 7 6 5 4 3 2 1

Year   2022 2021 2020 2019 2018

Cover photo © Nigel Spooner/Alamy Stock Photo
Illustrations by Integra Software Services
Typeset in Bembo Std Regular 10.75/12.75 by Integra Software Services Pvt. Ltd., Pondicherry, India
Printed in India

A catalogue record for this title is available from the British Library.

My Revision Planner

REVISED

Introduction

Unit 3: Thematic study and historical interpretation

Unit 3 in the OCR A-level specification involves the thematic study over a period of at least 100 years, and three in-depth studies of events, individuals or issues that are key parts of the theme. You will be expected to view the theme synoptically. In other words, you should be able to make links between events over the whole period. You will need to be able to compare and contrast developments over the period and make judgements based on your observations. In the in-depth studies section of the paper, you will be expected to apply your knowledge to two interpretations, evaluate them, and reach a supported judgement on which interpretation you consider to be the most valid.

Rebellion and Disorder under the Tudors 1485–1603

The following is a list of the main key topics you will study within the theme.
- **Key Topic 1:** The main causes of rebellion and disorder
- **Key Topic 2:** The frequency and nature of disturbances
- **Key Topic 3:** The impact of disturbances on Tudor governments
- **Key Topic 4:** The maintenance of political stability

The depth studies topics are:
- The Pilgrimage of Grace
- The Western Rebellion
- Tyrone's rebellion

Examination requirements

The exam lasts two and a half hours. You are advised to spend an hour on Section A, and one and a half hours on Section B, which will give you 45 minutes for each essay.

The A-level examination at the end of the course includes all the content.

You are required to answer **one** in-depth question, for which there is **no** choice, and **two** thematic essays from a choice of **three**.

At A-level Unit 3 will be worth a total of 80 marks and 40 per cent of the A-level.

In the A-level examination you are being tested on:
- the ability to use relevant historical information
- the skill of analysing factors and reaching a judgement.

How to use this book

This book has been designed to help you develop the knowledge and skills necessary to succeed in the examination.
- The book is divided into seven sections – one for each key topic of the thematic element and one for each of the in-depth topics.
- Each section is made up of a series of topics organised into double-page spreads.
- On the left-hand page you will find a summary of the key content you will need to learn. Words in bold in the key content are defined in the glossary (see pages 98–101)
- On the right-hand page you will find exam-focused activities.

Together these two strands of the book will provide you with the knowledge and skills essential for examination success.

▼ **Key historical content**

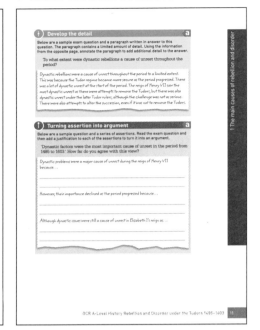

▼ **Exam-focused activities**

Examination activities

There are three levels of exam-focused activities:

- Band 1 activities are designed to develop the foundation skills needed to pass the exam. These have a green heading and this symbol.
- Band 2 activities are designed to build on the skills developed in Band 1 activities and to help you to achieve a C grade. These have an orange heading and this symbol.
- Band 3 activities are designed to enable you to access the highest grades. These have a purple heading and this symbol.

Some of the activities have answers or suggested answers that can be found online at www.hoddereducation.co.uk/myrevisionnotes. These have the following symbol to indicate this.

Each section ends with exam-style questions and sample answers with examiner's commentary. This will give you guidance on what is expected to achieve the top grade.

You can also keep track of your revision by ticking off each topic heading in the book, or by ticking the checklist on the contents page. Tick each box when you have:

- revised and understood a topic
- completed the activities.

Mark schemes

For some of the activities in the book it will be useful to refer to the A Level mark schemes for this paper. These have been abbreviated below.

Level	Historical interpretation	Thematic essay
6	Well-focused answer, aware of the wider debate with detailed knowledge used to evaluate the interpretations and reach a judgement. [26–30]	Very good focus and clear argument with developed synthesis across the period to reach a substantiated judgement. [21–25]
5	Good focus, with some awareness of the wider debate and uses good knowledge to evaluate the interpretations and reach a judgement. [21–25]	Good focus and argument with some synthesis across the period to reach a developed judgement. [17–20]
4	Mostly focused with awareness of the wider debate and uses some knowledge to evaluate the interpretations and produce a judgement. [16–20]	Mostly focused argument with limited synthesis across the period to reach a limited judgement. [13–16]
3	Partially focused with limited awareness of the wider debate and limited knowledge used to evaluate the interpretations. [11–15]	Partial focus and argument with undeveloped synthesis across the period to reach a judgement which is poorly supported. [9–12]
2	Limited focus and awareness of the wider debate and uses limited knowledge to evaluate but relies on information from the passages. [6–10]	Limited focus and argument with a judgement which is not well linked to the explanation. [5–8]
1	More on the topic with description of the interpretations. [1–5]	Limited focus on the topic and is mostly descriptive with a judgement that is asserted. [1–4]

Rebellion and disorder under the Tudors: An overview

There were a large number of rebellions throughout the Tudor period and every Tudor monarch faced challenges from some of their subjects. However, most of the population obeyed the demands of the state. Over the whole Tudor period probably no more than 80,000 Englishmen actively rebelled, from a total population of some 15 million.

Regardless of the question you are answering, you will need to know details of the main rebellions in both England and Ireland and use them as examples of the causes and nature of rebellions and the governments' response to them as it attempted to maintain stability. The main rebellions are outlined on these two pages.

Henry VII (1485–1509)

Henry VII, a Lancastrian, faced five major challenges to his throne. He had won the crown in 1485 at the Battle of Bosworth, but the defeated Yorkist family launched a number of rebellions to try to regain the throne.

Lovell and Stafford Rebellion (1486)

The first came within a year of Henry's accession with the Lovell and Stafford Rebellion in 1486. Francis Viscount Lovell and Humphrey Stafford, councillors to Richard III and Yorkists, had avoided capture at the Battle of Bosworth, took sanctuary at Colchester and escaped and raised troops in an attempt to overthrow Henry. The rebellion failed, Lovell fled to Flanders and Stafford was executed.

Simnel rebellion (1486–87)

Soon after this, in 1486–87, Henry faced the Simnel rebellion. Lambert Simnel claimed to be the Yorkist Earl of Warwick, who had a better claim to the throne than Henry as the son of the Duke of Clarence and cousin to Edward V. Although he had some English and Irish noble support he was defeated at the Battle of East Stoke.

Yorkshire (1489) and Cornish (1497) Rebellions

The next two rebellions were over taxation. First, Yorkshire rebelled in 1489 over funding a war in France. The rebels killed the Earl of Northumberland, who had been sent to collect the tax, before being defeated. Then, in 1497, Cornwall rebelled over taxes to fight the Scots. Although the Cornish rebels marched to London, they were slaughtered at Blackheath, the leaders were executed and the county was fined.

Warbeck's rebellion (1491–97)

Perkin Warbeck's rebellion lasted from 1491 until 1497. He claimed to be Richard, Duke of York – one of the Princes in the Tower. He won support from some nobles and, at times, from foreign powers. However, his attempted invasion in 1497 ended in defeat in the West Country. He was captured and executed in 1499.

Henry VIII (1509–47)

Although seen as the most powerful Tudor monarch, Henry faced three rebellions, two of which were large scale.

The Amicable Grant Rising (1525)

The Amicable Grant Rising in 1525 was a response to the heavy tax demands to fund the war in France. The scale of the rising, which involved large numbers of peasants and had some noble sympathy, engulfed much of East Anglia and parts of the home counties and midlands, and forced the government to abandon the tax.

The Silken Thomas Rebellion (1534–37)

The Silken Thomas Rebellion was an Irish rebellion that followed the arrest and imprisonment of the father of Thomas O'Neill (also known as Silken Thomas), the Earl of Kildare. The Kildare family had acted as the crown's deputy in Ireland, but had begun to be replaced by English officials. The rebels were defeated and executed.

The Pilgrimage of Grace (1536–37)

Three separate risings in the north of England in 1536–37, usually referred to as the Pilgrimage of Grace, were a reaction to the religious changes of the **Reformation**, as well as underlying social and economic grievances. The rebel force numbered some 40,000 at its height and Henry was forced to 'play for time' by negotiating with the rebels, before going back on his promises and executing over 200 rebels.

Edward VI (1547–53)

Two large-scale rebellions and a series of smaller risings have led to 1549 being known as the 'commotion time'.

The Western Rebellion (1549)

The Western Rebels besieged Exeter and wanted an end to the Protestant reforms, as well as an end to taxes on sheep and wool. It took the government five battles to finally defeat them at the battle of Clyst Heath.

Kett's rebellion (1549)

Kett's rebellion in Norfolk was largely social and economic. The rebels established a series of camps, even capturing Norwich, and were only defeated at the Battle of Dussindale.

Smaller riots

Meanwhile, most of central and southern England witnessed smaller-scale risings, often about social and economic grievances, which the local **gentry** and nobility were able to control.

Mary Tudor (1553–58)

Although Mary faced a challenge from Lady Jane Grey before she was able to take the throne, she faced only one other rebellion during her reign, despite the supposed unpopularity of her religious policy and the burning of many Protestants.

Lady Jane Grey (1553)

Mary's accession to the throne was initially successfully challenged by the Lord President of the Council, the Duke of Northumberland. He succeeded in having his daughter-in-law Lady Jane Grey crowned. She was the great-niece of Henry VIII and granddaughter of his sister Mary, making her the next in line to the throne if Mary Tudor and Elizabeth were excluded. However, Mary Tudor raised a force and Northumberland submitted without a fight after nine days. Lady Jane Grey was executed.

Wyatt's rebellion (1554)

The second challenge to Mary came from Thomas Wyatt in Kent. It was initially planned as a four-pronged attack on London to prevent Mary's marriage to Philip of Spain. The rebels feared England would be dominated by Spaniards and there would be a re-established Catholic dynasty. Wyatt was the only rebel who was able to raise troops (he raised 5000 men) and reached Ludgate (London), where he was finally arrested and later executed.

Elizabeth I (1558–1603)

Although the number of rebellions in England declined dramatically in the second half of the Tudor period, with Elizabeth facing only three rebellions in over 40 years, the situation in Ireland was very different.

Irish rebellions

- Shane O'Neill rose in 1558, resentful at losing the earldom of Tyrone to his brother. The rebellion ended only in 1567 when he was killed in inter-clan fighting.
- The Fitzgerald or Munster Rebellion (1569–73) was a response to English plantations in Munster. It started as a private war between the Earls of Desmond and Ormonde, but Desmond's cousin appealed for foreign help and this worried Elizabeth. Although this unrest was quickly put down, it led to further unrest against the plantation system. James Fitzgerald fled to Rome, but he returned to lead a second rebellion (the Geraldine) 1579. This time the protests were about increased English control and the imposition of religious reform. Although Fitzgerald was killed, his brother succeeded him as Earl of Desmond and took over the rebellion until defeated and executed in 1583.
- The final Irish rebellion, led by Hugh O'Neill, Earl of Tyrone, lasted from 1595 to 1603. This large-scale rising saw much of Ireland in arms against English rule and there were several English defeats, for example at Yellow Ford in 1598. It was only when Elizabeth sent sufficient forces, under Lord Mountjoy, that the rebellion was crushed.

English rebellions

- The most serious English rebellion, with 5000 men, was that of the Northern Earls in 1569. Northumberland and Westmorland planned to marry Mary Queen of Scots to the Duke of Norfolk and force Elizabeth to name her as heir to the throne. However, the rebellion got little support and most rebels fled as the royal army approached. Northumberland was executed, but Westmorland was not caught.
- The Oxfordshire rising of 1596 over enclosure is best remembered for its abject failure. Only four rebels turned up, but this did not prevent the government from executing all of them.
- The final challenge to Elizabeth came from a courtier and former favourite, the Earl of Essex. His attempt in 1601 to raise London against the dominance of the Cecil faction lasted only twelve hours. Essex was captured and executed.

1 The main causes of rebellion and disorder

Dynastic succession

REVISED

The **Yorkist** defeat at Bosworth and their replacement by the Tudors brought about dynastic unrest. This was a major cause of rebellion at the start of the period as the Yorkists attempted to remove Henry VII and the desire to remove the Tudors or change the succession remained a cause of unrest throughout the period 1485–1603.

Henry VII, 1485–1509

Henry's reign saw the most frequent and serious dynastic challenges because his claim to the throne was weak. He had won the throne in battle and was a **usurper**. Although he had killed Richard III, there were other Yorkists with a stronger claim to the throne and the issue of the succession caused three major rebellions during his reign.

Lovell and Stafford, 1486

Viscount Lovell, one of Richard's former councillors, and the Yorkists, Humphrey and Thomas Stafford, raised troops to kill Henry as he went on progress to his northern capital, York. They wanted to replace him with a leading Yorkist, either the Earl of Warwick or de la Pole.

Lambert Simnel, 1487

An Oxford priest, Richard Symonds, claimed Simnel, his pupil, was the Earl of Warwick. Warwick was a nephew of Richard III and been imprisoned by Henry. The conspiracy was supported by Yorkists, including the Earl of Lincoln, Lovell and Edward IV's sister, Margaret of Burgundy. Margaret paid for 2000 Irish **mercenaries**, but the conspiracy failed to gain support when they landed in England. Henry defeated the rebels at East Stoke. Despite his victory, it showed the fate of the crown could still be decided by battle.

Perkin Warbeck, 1491–97

Warbeck pretended to be the Duke of York, another of Richard's nephews, but he had probably been murdered when Richard seized the throne. He gained foreign support from France, Burgundy and Scotland. But because of Henry's successful foreign policy alliances, Warbeck's attempts to invade failed. The first attempted invasion at Deal in 1495 led to his flight to Ireland then Scotland. His attempt to invade from Scotland in 1496 failed, and in 1497 he attempted to land in south-west England, but was captured.

The importance of the succession as a cause of rebellion declined in the rest of the period.

Henry VIII: The Pilgrimage of Grace, 1536–37

The succession was not a main cause, but the rebels wanted the restoration of Henry VIII's daughter, Mary, to the succession having been declared illegitimate after her mother, **Catherine of Aragon**'s, divorce from Henry.

Mary Tudor, 1553–58

Lady Jane Grey, 1553 coup

The dying Edward VI drew up the **Devise** to exclude Mary from the succession in favour of **Lady Jane Grey**, daughter-in-law of Northumberland, **Lord President of the Council**. Jane was crowned, but Mary as the legitimate ruler gained support and the Duke of Northumberland surrendered after nine days.

Wyatt, 1554

A courtier and member of the Kentish gentry, **Thomas Wyatt** attempted to secure the succession of Elizabeth. He attempted to stop Mary's marriage to Philip of Spain, which would prevent Elizabeth's succession if the marriage produced children. The rebellion was stopped at the gates of the city of London.

Elizabeth I, 1558–1603

The Northern Earls, 1569

The earls rebelled to ensure that Mary Queen of Scots was heir if Elizabeth died childless. They wanted Mary to marry the **Duke of Norfolk** and for Elizabeth to name her heir, which would also ensure a Catholic succession.

Essex, 1601

The Earl of Essex wanted to force Elizabeth to acknowledge James VI of Scotland as heir. He hoped this would gain him James' favour. He also wanted Elizabeth to remove other councillors so he was the 'kingmaker'.

Develop the detail a

Below are a sample exam question and a paragraph written in answer to this question. The paragraph contains a limited amount of detail. Using the information from the opposite page, annotate the paragraph to add additional detail to the answer.

To what extent were dynastic rebellions a cause of unrest throughout the period?

Dynastic rebellions were a cause of unrest throughout the period to a limited extent. This was because the Tudor regime became more secure as the period progressed. There was a lot of dynastic unrest at the start of the period. The reign of Henry VII saw the most dynastic unrest as there were attempts to remove the Tudors, but there was also dynastic unrest under the later Tudor rulers, although the challenge was not as serious. There were also attempts to alter the succession, even if it was not to remove the Tudors.

Turning assertion into argument a

Below are a sample question and a series of assertions. Read the exam question and then add a justification to each of the assertions to turn it into an argument.

'Dynastic factors were the most important cause of unrest in the period from 1485 to 1603.' How far do you agree with this view?

Dynastic problems were a major cause of unrest during the reign of Henry VII because...

_____

_____

However, their importance declined as the period progressed because...

_____

_____

Although dynastic issues were still a cause of unrest in Elizabeth I's reign as...

_____

_____

Taxation

> For a description of all the rebellions mentioned see pages 8–9.

Taxation was the single most important cause of unrest in the early Tudor period. People objected to increased or **innovative taxation** demands, either because new demands indicated unwelcome increased control from central government, or because people simply could not afford to pay.

It was the main cause of unrest in the revolts of 1489, 1497 and 1525 and a minor cause in 1536 and 1549. After 1549 it was not an issue, although the heavy tax demands caused by the Spanish war may have played a role in the Oxfordshire rising of 1596 (see page 20).

Henry VII, 1485–1509

Henry's weak position and dynastic threats meant he needed to raise money to secure his position. In 1489 parliament voted for £100,000 in taxation to fund a war in France and in 1497 they voted an additional £60,000 to fund a war against the Scots. This led to regional rebellions from Yorkshire and Cornwall, as they objected to paying taxes to fund wars which did not concern them, indicating that **provincialism** was strong in England.

Yorkshire rebellion, 1489

Protestors in Yorkshire objected to paying for a war in France that did not concern them and from which they were traditionally exempt because they had to pay for defence of the northern borders against the Scots. The north was also very poor and the situation was made worse by a bad harvest in 1488. Henry refused to negotiate, despite other northern counties being excluded from the tax due to their poverty, and the rebels murdered the tax collector, the Earl of Northumberland. An army was sent, which easily defeated the rebels.

Cornish rising, 1497

As in Yorkshire, the Cornish objected to paying for wars that did not concern them, this time against the Scots and **Perkin Warbeck** (see page 10). The rebels claimed their grievances were against royal officials who advised the king on finance, **John Morton** and **Reginald Bray**. The threat was serious as the rebels raised 15,000 men and marched to Blackheath in London. A royal army was sent and the rebels were defeated.

Henry VIII, 1509–47

The Amicable Grant rising, 1525

The Amicable Grant was a **non-parliamentary tax** which followed a period of heavy taxation as England was at war with France. Having raised **forced loans** in 1522 and a **subsidy** in 1523, many people were financially exhausted and there had been little territorial gain in Henry's earlier wars in the 1510s. The grant was based on assessments made by government officials and ended the concept of a **fixed rate** so that many were paying taxes at a higher rate than previously. It also came at a time of worsening economic conditions. There were protests in many counties, but larger risings in Suffolk. The difficulty in collecting the money forced the government to back down and the ringleaders were pardoned.

The Pilgrimage of Grace, 1536–37

Only one of the rebels' **articles** in the Pilgrimage of Grace (see page 74) concerned taxation. They demanded that the **Subsidy Act** of 1534 was abandoned. The rebels argued that the tax was innovative as it was not being raised for the defence of the realm.

Edward VI: The Western Rebellion, 1549

The Western Rebellion in 1549 (see page 82) opposed the Subsidy Act of 1549 which aimed to raise money on sheep and woollen cloth. This would have hit farmers in the West Country particularly hard, where sheep farming predominated. It was made worse because the tax would be assessed just after the introduction of the new **Prayer Book**, which was also resented.

Spot the mistake

Below are a sample exam question and a paragraph written in answer to this question. Why does this paragraph not get into at least Level 5? Once you have identified the mistake, rewrite the paragraph so that it displays the qualities of at least Level 5. The mark scheme on page 7 will help you.

'Taxation was the most important cause of social and economic unrest in the period from 1485 to 1603.' How far do you agree?

Taxation caused the Yorkshire rising in 1489. The rebels objected to paying taxes to fund Henry VII's war in France. The northern counties were usually exempt from such taxes as they were expected to pay for the defence of the northern borders against Scottish attacks. They also felt that the war against France did not concern them and therefore the tax was unfair. Yorkshire also objected as other northern counties had been exempted from the tax because of poverty.

Mind map

Use the information on the opposite page to add detail to the mind map below.

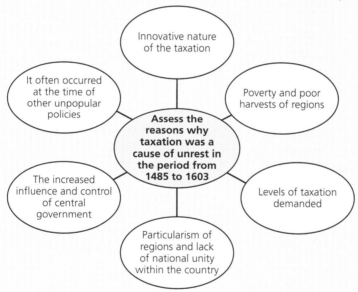

- Innovative nature of the taxation
- It often occurred at the time of other unpopular policies
- Poverty and poor harvests of regions
- **Assess the reasons why taxation was a cause of unrest in the period from 1485 to 1603**
- The increased influence and control of central government
- Levels of taxation demanded
- Particularism of regions and lack of national unity within the country

Religion

> For a description of all the rebellions mentioned see pages 8–9.

Religion became a cause of rebellion as a result of the Reformation. Until the 1530s religion had been a unifying factor, helping to increase political stability, but it was a major cause of two rebellions and played a role of varying importance in four other rebellions in the period between 1536 and 1569. Most rebellions with religion as a cause wanted to reverse the religious changes, with Kett's being the exception. However, by the end of the period it was no longer a cause of unrest as most people accepted the Elizabethan Church.

Henry VIII: The Pilgrimage of Grace, 1536–37

The Pilgrimage comprised three separate risings in northern England. They were in response to **visitations** by Church commissioners to investigate the clergy and close smaller monasteries. This also caused rumours of attacks on parish churches. The rebels argued that the closure of the monasteries affected not only religious provision, but the social and economic services provided by them. In addition, monasteries often acted as the church for local people and their closure would have had an impact on local church attendance. The rebel demands reflected this concern. Nine of the twenty-four demands were about religious grievances, including the attack on saints, holy days and pilgrimages as well as monasteries. The rising had many religious symbols with the rebels carrying a banner of the **Five Wounds of Christ** and singing the **Pilgrims' ballad**.

Edward VI, 1547–53

The Western Rebellion, 1549

As well as its economic causes (see page 82) the Western Rebellion seemed to be a reaction to the changes brought about by the Edwardian reformation, particularly the introduction of the 1549 Prayer Book. Thirteen demands were religious and called for a restoration of traditional Catholic practices: the Latin mass, **relics**, images and **chantries**. However, they did not call for the restoration of the **papacy**.

Kett's rebellion, 1549

Although largely a social protest (see page 18), the rebels did complain about the lack of progress of the Reformation and called for an improvement in the quality of the clergy.

Mary I, 1553–58

Lady Jane Grey coup, 1553

Although the **coup** to place Lady Jane Grey on the throne was largely political (see page 10), it could be argued that the leaders of the coup were concerned that Mary's accession would lead to a Catholic restoration and therefore rose to defend the changes brought about under Edward.

Wyatt's rebellion, 1554

Thomas Wyatt claimed the rising was not religious, but this may have been an attempt to widen support to include Catholics opposed to Mary's marriage. However, it took place in a strongly Protestant area and people knew that Mary was a staunch Catholic. There were fears her marriage would result in the re-establishment of a Catholic dynasty.

Elizabeth I: The Northern Earls, 1569

The Earl of Northumberland claimed the first aim was to reform religion. Indeed, the two leaders, Northumberland and Westmorland, were both Catholic. However, it may well have been a cloak for political motives. Nevertheless, there were many religious elements, with the rebels using the banner of the Five Wounds, restoring mass in Durham Cathedral, destroying **English Bibles** and setting up **stone altars**.

Develop the detail

a

Below are a sample exam question and paragraph written in answer to this question. The paragraph contains a limited amount of detail. Annotate the paragraph to add additional detail to the answer.

'Religion was the most common cause of rebellion in England throughout the period 1485–1603.' How far do you agree with this view?

Religion was a cause of rebellion only during the middle part of the period. It was only when Henry VIII introduced religious changes that it became a cause of unrest as before then the country was religiously united. Religion was a particularly important cause of the Pilgrimage of Grace under Henry VIII, although there were other causes of this rebellion as well. It continued to be an important cause of rebellion under Edward VI, most notably in the Western Rebellion, where the rebels wanted to reverse the changes he had introduced. However, it was also a minor cause of Kett's rebellion, where the rebels complained about the clergy. The last rebellion where religion was important was the rebellion of the Northern Earls, who had similar religious symbols as the Pilgrims and restored traditional practices. However, after this rebellion religion played no further role in causing unrest, unlike other factors which remained a cause throughout the period.

Introducing an argument

Below are a sample exam question, a list of key points to be made in the essay, and a simple introduction and conclusion for the essay. Read the question, the key points and the introduction and conclusion. Using the information on the opposite page, earlier in the section and on page 16, rewrite the introduction and the conclusion in order to develop an argument.

Assess the reasons why religion was a cause of unrest only in the period from 1536 to 1569.

Key points:

- Lack of noticeable religious change before 1536
- Preserve traditional practices
- Link to succession and **faction**
- **Elizabethan Church Settlement**
- Cloak for political motives

Introduction:

There were many reasons why religion was a cause of unrest only in the period from 1536 to 1569. These reasons were linked to politics, faction and the succession as well as religious issues. It is also important to consider why there was no religious unrest in the periods before 1536 and after 1569. This was because of the lack of religious change. All of these factors help to explain why religion was a cause of unrest only between 1536 and 1569.

Conclusion:

To conclude, there were many reasons why religion was cause of unrest only in the period from 1536 to 1569. These reasons were linked to politics, faction and the succession as well as religious issues. The context in which the religious changes were made was also important. However, the most important reason was the nature of the religious changes in the period from 1536 to 1569.

For a description of all the rebellions mentioned see pages 8–9.

The emergence of a small group of councillors from whom the monarch took advice led to the development of factions. Councillors, whose advice was ignored, or who were not rewarded with **patronage**, formed opposition groups and tried to replace those in positions of influence. This was possibly the most common cause of unrest throughout the period and can be found as a cause of most rebellions, although often as a secondary, rather than primary cause. These factions turned to rebellion when all other attempts to achieve influence had failed.

Henry VII, 1485–1509

Although associated with dynastic unrest (see page 10), the Yorkists (the Lovell, Stafford and **Pretender** risings) acted like a faction. They wanted to remove both the king and the 'evil councillors', such as Bray and Morton (see page 12), who advised him.

Henry VIII, 1509–47

The Amicable Grant rising, 1525

It has been suggested that a major cause of the failure to raise the Amicable Grant was factional as those opposed to Cardinal **Wolsey**, who dominated the court, used the original opposition to the tax to stir up further unrest and made little effort to collect the tax. This allowed opposition to spread and opponents of Wolsey hoped that Henry would lose faith in his minister.

The Pilgrimage of Grace, 1536–37

It has been argued that the motivation behind the Pilgrimage of Grace was factional. The **Aragonese** faction, supporters of Catherine of Aragon and her daughter, wanted to regain influence. The rebellion attempted to remove Henry's chief minister, **Thomas Cromwell**. Many of the leaders, such as **Lord Thomas Darcy** and **Lord John Hussey**, had links with Catherine. They hoped to restore Mary to the succession.

Mary I, 1553–58

Lady Jane Grey coup, 1553

It could be argued that the attempt to alter the succession in favour of Lady Jane Grey (see page 10) was an attempt to preserve the domination of Northumberland's supporters, knowing they would lose influence when Mary came to the throne.

Wyatt's rebellion, 1554

Originally, the rebellion was supposed to be a four-pronged attack on the capital, led by many who would have lost, or feared they would lose, influence at court with the marriage of Mary to Philip of Spain. Men, such as Wyatt, who had served earlier monarchs, feared they would lose their positions and influence to Spaniards who would be rewarded following the marriage.

Elizabeth I, 1558–1603

The Northern Earls, 1569

Northumberland and Westmorland were losing influence both at court and in the north, as southern councillors, led by William Cecil, dominated court and were brought into government in the north. They blamed him for the religious changes and the foreign policy that appeared to be taking England closer to war, as well as causing uncertainty over the succession. This led to their plan to marry Mary Queen of Scots to the Duke of Norfolk and force Elizabeth to recognise her as heir.

The Earl of Essex, 1601

A former favourite of Elizabeth, the **Earl of Essex** had been suspended from the **Privy Council** and banned from court, where Robert Cecil dominated. His position was in decline and he was unable to provide rewards for his supporters such as the Earl of Southampton. He believed that a demonstration in London would have support and force Elizabeth to restore his influence.

Spectrum of significance

Below are a sample exam question and a list of general points which could be used to answer part of the question. Use information on the opposite page and from the rest of this section to reach a judgement about the importance of these general points to the question posed. Write numbers on the spectrum below to indicate their relative importance. Having done this, write a brief justification of your placement, explaining why some of these factors are more important than others. The resulting diagram could form the basis of an essay plan.

'Faction was the most important cause of unrest throughout the period from 1485 to 1603.' How far do you agree with this view?

1 Faction

2 Heavy taxation

3 Religious changes

4 Dynastic challenges to the throne

5 Economic and social problems

6 Increased government centralisation

←——————————————————————————————→

Least important   Most important

Developing an argument

Read the following sample exam question, a list of key points to be made in the essay, and a paragraph from the essay. Using the information from the opposite page and from earlier in this section, rewrite the paragraph in order to develop an argument. Your paragraph should explain why the factor discussed in the paragraph is either the most significant factor or less significant than another factor.

'Faction was the most serious cause of unrest throughout the period 1485–1603.' How far do you agree?

Key points:

- Factional disputes threatened every Tudor monarch *but*
- Attracted limited support
- Dynastic unrest forced the monarch into battle
- Taxation rebellions often attracted large numbers and forced a change in policy

Sample paragraph:

Factional unrest affected every Tudor monarch. Henry VII faced challenges from the Yorkist faction following his victory at Bosworth. Simnel and his 3000 mercenaries fought Henry at Stoke and there was further factional conflict with Warbeck and Lovell and Stafford. There were also taxation rebellions in Yorkshire and Cornwall. These rebellions forced the government to abandon the taxes. Under Henry VIII the large-scale rising against the Amicable Grant was to prevent further taxes, but it also attacked the king's chief minister, Wolsey. The 40,000 who rose in the Pilgrimage of Grace were mostly concerned by religious changes but also attacked Cromwell and attempted to restore the influence of Catherine of Aragon's supporters. Wyatt's rebellion, which attracted 5000, was a response to the Spanish marriage and fears that courtiers would lose their positions. During Elizabeth's reign the Northern Earls rose with 5000 men, but fled when royal forces approached. Essex raised a few hundred men in his protest against his loss of influence. The city of London did not rise to support him.

Famine, inflation and social issues

REVISED ☐

> For a description of all the rebellions mentioned see pages 8–9.

Many of the riots throughout the period were the result of social and economic tensions. They were often the triggers for localised unrest and, if not put down quickly, could become major rebellions.

Famine and disease

Although one in four harvests failed and resulted in increased mortality and price rises, there is only one obvious example where this resulted in open rebellion – the Oxfordshire rising of 1596 (see page 20). However, there were examples of **food riots**, particularly during Elizabeth's reign in the 1580s and 1590s, with riots in Gloucestershire and Hampshire in 1586 and Somerset, Sussex and Kent in 1596–97.

Similarly, despite at least four outbreaks of plague and **the 'sweat'** there was no associated unrest.

It appears that in times of famine and disease potential rebels stayed at home to look after their crops, whilst the **yeomen** and **gentry**, who might have led unrest, benefited from the subsequent rise in the price of food.

Inflation and rents

Inflation was an increasing problem from the 1520s onwards and had a serious impact on the price of grain, which rose faster than wages. This was largely the result of a rising population which increased demand for grain. **Wage labourers** suffered the most and inflation did play a role in some rebellions in the mid-century. Landowners raised rents to try to make up for the losses caused by inflation and often evicted those who could not pay.

The Pilgrimage of Grace, 1536–37

The Pilgrims wanted **entry fines** to be set at two years' rent. This would prevent landlords making up for their losses from rents, caused by inflation, by charging more to new **tenants**. The rebels also argued that the closure of the monasteries would hit the poor who relied on monastic charity.

Kett's rebellion, 1549

The rebels had the unrealistic demand that the price of land and rent for land be returned to that of 1485. Similar to the Pilgrims, they also wanted entry fines to be controlled. Some landlords had also revived old feudal dues, such as **castleward**, which the rebels protested against.

Social issues

Social issues were a major cause of the unrest that gripped England in 1549, resulting in what has been described as 'commotion time' or 'camping time' as the rebels often established camps from which they attempted to control the local area. There was unrest in 26 counties in central and southern England. Social grievances were clearly present in the demands of both Kett's rebellion and the Western Rebels. It does appear that in both rebellions the rebels wanted to narrow the gap between the rich and the peasants.

Kett's rebellion, 1549

Seventeen of the twenty-nine demands were linked to rents, landlords and **enclosures** (see page 20). The rebels' targets were landlords and it was the closest thing to '**class war**' seen in this period, as most land was owned by a small number of nobles and gentry. The rebels wanted **serfs** to be set free and a number of the demands specifically attacked offices of local government, which were held by gentry. There were criticisms of rabbit warrens and dovecotes, again symbols of gentry status.

The Western Rebellion, 1549

Although there were no demands regarding rents, the rebels attacked gentry at St Michael's Mount and Trematon suggesting that class war was not far below the surface. The demands included a call to limit the size of gentry households.

Support or challenge?

Below is a sample exam question which asks how far you agree with a specific statement. Below this is a series of general statements which are relevant to the question. Using your own knowledge of the whole period and the information on the opposite page, decide whether these statements support or challenge the statement in the question and tick the appropriate box.

'A greater cause of unrest in the period up to 1549 than in the period from 1549 to 1603.' How far do you agree with this view of social problems as a cause of unrest?

	Support	Challenge
There was little unrest caused by social issues during the reign of Henry VII		
The Pilgrims demanded that entry fines were set at two years' rent		
Outbreaks of plague and sweat never directly caused unrest		
Kett's rebels wanted the price of land and rents to be returned to 1485 levels		
Unrest in 1549 affected 26 counties in southern and central England		
The Western Rebels attacked local gentry		
Food riots broke out in many areas of southern England in the 1580s and 1590s		
The only evidence of poor harvests causing unrest is the Oxfordshire rising of 1596		

 Introducing an argument

Read the following sample exam question, a list of key points to be made in the essay, and a simple introduction and conclusion for the essay. Using the information on the opposite page and from earlier in the section, rewrite the introduction and the conclusion in order to develop an argument.

'Rarely the trigger, but frequently the underlying cause.' How far do you agree with this view of the role of social and economic grievances as a cause of unrest in the period from 1485 to 1603?

Key points:
- What is meant by trigger and underlying cause
- Social grievances – class discontent
- Economic grievances – poor harvests, inflation, enclosure
- Trigger causes of unrest – enclosure, religious change, dynastic
- Underlying causes – inflation, religious change, poverty, faction

Introduction:

I partly agree that social and economic causes were rarely the trigger, but they were frequently the underlying cause of unrest. In some rebellions social and economic causes acted as the trigger, but in other rebellions other factors were more important. Social and economic grievances were often the underlying cause, but in some rebellions this was not the case.

Conclusion:

Social and economic grievances were rarely the trigger for unrest but often the underlying cause to an extent. They were not the trigger when class discontent caused unrest, but were when enclosure was a cause. They were important as underlying causes because of inflation and poor harvests, but religious changes and loss of influence were also important.

REVISED

> For a description of all the rebellions mentioned see pages 8–9.

Although enclosure was not often a major cause of unrest, it did cause tensions between landowners and tenants, particularly when land was converted from **arable** to **pasture**, resulting in less demand for labour, or where **common land** was fenced off. When this was done amicably there was little trouble. However, despite this, enclosure did play a role in the events of 1536, 1549 and 1596 and caused some local unrest in 1510.

Henry VIII: The Pilgrimage of Grace, 1536–37

One of the rebel demands called for the pulling down of enclosures put up since 1489, except in regions of mountains, forests and parks. There had been enclosure riots in 1535 and it was likely this was a grievance in certain areas of the north, particularly in lowlands where population had been rising and there was increased pressure on land.

Edward VI: The 'commotion time', 1549

Enclosure played a role in most of the 26 counties where unrest took place in 1549. It was a particular problem in the **sheep-corn areas** of the midlands, East Anglia and the south and south-east, where population pressure and land shortage added to the tensions. Encouraged by the **Duke of Somerset's Enclosure Commission**, many tenants took the law into their own hands and pulled down fences and hedges. The first rising, at Northaw in Hertfordshire, May 1548, was over enclosure and may have been the prelude to the other risings. This can be seen in the following examples:

- Wiltshire – Lord Herbert's hedges pulled down at Wilton.
- Sussex – Earl of Arundel forced some gentlemen to take down hedges to stop riots.
- Surrey – hedges at Witley Park pulled down.

Kett's rebellion, 1549

The first article of Kett's demands attacked enclosure and the rebellion was triggered by a dispute between landowners who had recently enclosed land, **Robert Kett** and **John Flowerdew**. Kett took down his own fences before the rebels did and led the attack on Flowerdew's lands. Landlords appeared to be obstructing an enquiry into illegal enclosure and the rebels may have believed that they would have government support in attacking enclosures. However, the demands were not simply anti-enclosure: the first demand protected enclosures where **saffron** was grown and many tenants supported enclosure when it prevented landowners from **folding cattle** on their land. The biggest concern was when wealthy landowners took over common land or pastured large flocks on it as it denied peasants the right.

The Western Rebellion, 1549

Although not mentioned in the demands, contemporaries did comment on the problem of enclosure and mentioned the pulling down of hedges.

Elizabeth I: The Oxfordshire rising, 1596

The government had lifted the restrictions on enclosing open fields in 1593 as there was plenty of cheap grain available. As a result, there were new enclosures in Oxfordshire at Hampton Gaye and Hampton Poyle. This was one of the reasons why an assembly was arranged at Enslow Hill in 1596, the site of the 1549 rising sparked by enclosures, but this time it failed to attract numbers and only four men appeared.

In 1607 the widespread midland enclosure revolt took place, indicating that enclosure was still an issue.

Identify an argument **a**

Below are a series of definitions, a sample exam question and two sample conclusions. One of the conclusions achieves a high level because it contains an argument. The other achieves a lower level because it contains only description and assertion. Identify which is which. The mark scheme on page 7 will help you.

- **Description:** a detailed account.
- **Assertion:** a statement of fact or an opinion which is not supported by a reason.
- **Reason:** a statement that explains or justifies something.
- **Argument:** an assertion justified with a reason.

How important was enclosure as a cause of unrest in the period from 1485–1603?

Sample 1:

> Enclosure was not a major cause of rebellion, but it did cause tensions, particularly when landowners encroached on common land or converted land from arable to pasture. Enclosure caused local riots, as in the 1510s, 1540s and 1590s, however only a few became serious, particularly in 1549. Enclosure was a major cause of Kett's rebellion in 1549, when the rebels threw down the hedges of John Flowerdew, and some of the other minor disturbances, as at Witley. However, in 1536 complaint against enclosure was only one of the grievances of the Pilgrims, whereas in 1596 only four people rose in Oxfordshire over enclosure grievances. Enclosure may have been an underlying grievance, but it was rarely the major cause of unrest.

Sample 2:

> There had been much rioting in the north over enclosure in 1535. Enclosure then appeared as a grievance in the list of demands drawn up by the Pilgrims in 1536. Kett's rebellion followed rivalry between two landowners, Robert Kett and John Flowerdew. Both had enclosed lands, but Kett pulled his down; he then led men to attack Flowerdew's fences. There were also further examples of hedges being pulled down in Surrey and the Home Counties. In 1593 the government lifted the restrictions on enclosing open fields, but in 1596, following enclosure in Oxfordshire, four men gathered at Enslow Hill. These events show that enclosure was a frequent cause of unrest throughout the period.

Turning assertion into argument **a**

Below are a sample exam question and a series of assertions. Read the exam question and then add a justification to each of the assertions to turn each one into an argument.

Assess the importance of enclosure as a cause of social and economic unrest in the period from 1485 to 1603.

> Enclosure was a significant cause of social and economic unrest because it led to…
>
> _____
>
> However, in many social and economic rebellions enclosure was often just the trigger because…
>
> _____
>
> Also, enclosure unrest often failed to raise large numbers because…
>
> _____

Ireland

> For a description of all the rebellions mentioned see pages 8–9.

The revolts in Ireland were largely the result of attempts by the government in England to increase central control. In that sense they were similar to the tax revolts of 1489, 1497 and 1525 (see page 12) and the Pilgrims in 1536 and Northern Earls (1569). Like Ireland, they felt that their traditional rights and privileges were being ignored.

Until 1534 the monarch had worked with the **Earl of Kildare**, who was **Deputy Lieutenant**, and there were no rebellions. However, the period from 1534–1603 saw five major rebellions (see pages 8–9), all primarily caused by increased government intervention.

Henry VIII, 1509–47

From 1532 onwards Thomas Cromwell, the king's chief minister, began to change the distribution of power in Ireland and Kildare started to lose influence. The crucial issues were the religious changes that followed Henry VIII's position as Head of the Church. The king doubted Kildare would enforce his new title. Kildare was summoned to England, but lodged in the Tower where he died, which prompted his son and uncles to rise in rebellion.

The Silken Thomas Rebellion, 1534

Kildare's son, **Thomas FitzGerald** (also known as **Silken Thomas**), ignored similar requests to come to London to discuss policy and instead raised 1000 men and invaded the **Pale**. Although the rebels attacked the religious changes, the primary cause of the unrest was political as Silken wanted to drive the English out and become ruler in Ireland.

Elizabeth I, 1558–1603

It was during the reign of Elizabeth that the majority of Irish rebellions occurred as the government attempted to increase its influence in Ireland and reduce the power of the **clan** chiefs.

Although all the rebellions were politically motivated against increased English control, religion and the defence of the Catholic Church were often used to gain wider support.

Shane O'Neill, 1558–67

O'Neill wanted to rule **Ulster** and killed his own brother to achieve it. Elizabeth forgave him, but he was soon plotting with France and Mary Queen of Scots. Although he claimed to be acting as defender of the Catholic faith, his aim was to increase his power.

Fitzgerald Rebellion, 1569–73

James Fitzmaurice Fitzgerald resented English attempts to colonise Ireland, where the settlers treated the Irish brutally, and the imposition of **martial law**, both of which increased English influence. He was particularly annoyed that his cousin had been put in the Tower following a feud with the English Butler clan. Although he also claimed to be defending Catholicism from Elizabeth's religious changes, it was the growing English influence that was the main cause.

Fitzgerald Rebellion, 1579–83

The main cause of unrest was the hatred towards the increasing number of English settlers and increased government interference from Dublin into clan life. However, in order to increase support, Fitzgerald also appealed to the growing animosity to the religious changes that had followed Elizabeth's **excommunication** and the 1569–73 rebellion.

Tyrone, 1595–1603

The **plantation system** caused increased hostility between the Irish and the English as the settlers raised rents, took over more land and began to establish the Protestant Church. In 1595 Hugh O'Neill, **Earl of Tyrone**, led a revolt, which soon became nationwide, with the aim of removing the settlers and the English administration so that Ireland became independent. Tyrone also had his own personal grievance as he felt he had not been properly rewarded by the English government for helping them when the government in Ireland was attacked by other clans.

Simple essay style

Below is a sample exam question. Use your own knowledge, information on the opposite page and information from other sections of the book to produce a plan for this question. Choose four general points, and provide three pieces of specific information to support each general point. Once you have planned your essay, write the introduction and conclusion for the essay. The introduction should list the points to be discussed in the essay **and outline the line of argument you intend to take**. The conclusion should summarise the key points and justify which point was the most important.

> To what extent were the causes of Irish rebellion similar to those in England in the period from 1485 to 1603?

 Recommended reading

Irish rebellions are often neglected by students. However, it is worth spending time studying them in some depth as it enhances understanding of patterns of change and continuity. Below is a list of suggested further reading on this topic.

- Steven G. Ellis, *Ireland in the Age of the Tudors*, Longman (1998)
- Barbara Mervyn, *Advanced History Core Texts: The Reign of Elizabeth, England 1558–1603*, Hodder Education (2001), pages 93–100
- John Warren, *Access to History: Elizabeth I: Religion and Foreign Affairs*, Hodder Education (2002), Chapter 6
- Geoff Woodward and Nicholas Fellows, *Access to History: Rebellion and Disorder under the Tudors 1485–1603*, Hodder Education (2016), pages 10–11, 22–24

Exam focus

Below is a sample high-level essay in response to an exam-style question. Read the essay and the comments around it.

How far did the causes of rebellion in England remain the same throughout the period 1485–1603?

The causes of rebellion under the Tudors centred on four main areas: dynastic and factional, taxation and religion. However, by the 'commotion time' of 1549 economic grievances, particularly those regarding enclosures, came to the forefront and were maintained until the end of the period, with the Oxfordshire rising of 1596.

A clear line of argument and there is some awareness of the need to address continuity and change.

Throughout the period dynastic rebellions were present with attempts to overthrow the monarch. This was seen in the Simnel and Warbeck rebellions, which attempted to remove Henry VII, in the Devise of 1553, when Edward VI attempted to exclude Mary and replace her with Lady Jane Grey, and the Northern Earls who wanted to replace Elizabeth with Mary Queen of Scots. This contrasts with attempts to amend the succession in 1536, when the Pilgrims wanted to restore Mary Tudor to the succession and the Essex rebellion which wanted to ensure the succession of James VI. Dynastic rebellions were therefore present throughout the period, but were most abundant during the reign of Henry VII, who was not secure following his seizure of the throne at Bosworth. However, unlike later rebellions these attempted to topple the Tudor regime by securing the throne using Pretenders, such as Warbeck and Simnel. However, the attempts made by Wyatt in 1554 and Westmorland and Northumberland in 1569 put forward legal claimants: Elizabeth and Mary Queen of Scots, respectively. The Earl of Essex's rebellion in 1601 also conformed to this pattern as he wanted to secure the throne for James VI of Scotland.

The opening sentence shows a link back to the question. There is evidence of synthesis and a good awareness of continuity and change, suggesting the response is likely to reach the higher levels.

Factional rebellions were present throughout the period, but the nature of the causes changed. During the reign of Henry VII factional unrest resulted in attempts by Yorkists to overthrow the monarch and restore the House of York, through attempts by Lovell, Stafford and the Pretenders. However, later factional rebellions, although caused by the loss of power and influence, did not attempt to overthrow the monarch, but restore the influence of the group that had lost favour. In the Amicable Grant unrest Norfolk and Suffolk exploited it to attack Wolsey and in 1536 the Pilgrims demanded that Cromwell and Rich should be punished and attempted to restore the influence of Catherine of Aragon's supporters. However, as the period progressed factionalism became entangled with religion. The 1553 Devise was as much an attempt to preserve Protestantism as it was to secure Northumberland's power, and Wyatt's rebellion aimed to preserve Protestantism by preventing Mary's marriage to Philip, as it was an attempt to prevent a Spanish-dominated court. Despite this, most factional rebellions were attempts by individuals or groups to reassert their fading power, seen with both the Aragonese faction in 1536 and Northumberland and Westmorland in 1569, who had lost influence in the north. Similarly, Essex rebelled as he had lost his political influence with the rise of Robert Cecil.

The opening sentence links directly to the question. The paragraph shows the continuity of faction as a cause, although it does note how the nature changes. There is evidence of synthesis with comparisons and evidence of similarity.

Taxation rebellions were largely a feature of the reigns of Henry VII and Henry VIII. However, Somerset's 1549 statutes for taxes on Sheep and Cloth added to the grievances of the Western Rebels. Similarly, the high taxes resulting from the conflict against Spain contributed to the Oxfordshire rising, suggesting that taxation was a consistent, albeit subsidiary, cause in the second half of the period. Throughout the reigns of Henry VII and Henry VIII tax rebellions followed the introduction of innovative taxes to finance wars, against Scotland under Henry VII and France in 1525. Both the Cornish and Yorkshire revolts were in response to being asked to fund wars in regions that were not usually their responsibility. Tax remained an issue under Henry VIII, but this time protests were against the levels of taxation demanded by the Amicable Grant. Similarly in the Pilgrimage of Grace, the rebels objected to paying the 1534 subsidy because of the high demands, but also the poor harvests. Therefore, as with dynastic unrest, although taxation remained a cause throughout much of the period, the nature of the causes changed and taxation became a subsidiary issue.

The opening sentence again links back to the question and sets out a line of argument which is developed throughout the paragraph. There is synthesis as the response shows that causes were similar. The final sentence also links the material back to the question and reinforces the argument.

Economic and social issues were a more significant cause of unrest in the second half of the period; although the Pilgrims did complain about enclosures and entry fines in 1536, it was only a minor cause of the rising. Economic and social causes became more significant in 1549. They were a direct cause of both Kett and the Western Rebellion. Both rebellions complained about enclosures, provoked by Somerset's Enclosure Commission of 1548, and the actions of both sets of rebels, with their attacks on the gentry, such as Hellyons, suggests that class division was also a cause. Unrest in much of the rest of south and central England was also concerned with enclosure, suggesting that economic causes had become more important and remained so until the end of the period, with the Oxfordshire rising the result of enclosure. Therefore, although there had been economic causes in the earlier period, they were only underlying causes, but after 1548 they became more significant.

The opening sentence sets out the line of argument that is developed. The response is aware how economic causes went from being a subsidiary cause to a main cause.

Religion was a cause of rebellion only between 1536 and 1569. Religious change following the break with Rome caused unrest with protests against religious innovation and attempts to restore traditional practices. The Pilgrims, Western Rebels and Northern Earls all attempted to restore traditional Catholic practices. The Pilgrims complained about the attack on holy days, images and monasteries, the Western Rebels about the attack on images and chantries, whilst the Northern Earls attempted to restore the Catholic mass. However, perhaps the clearest sign of continuity was the use by all these rebels of the banner of the Five Wounds of Christ. The only exception to this attempt to restore traditional practices was Kett, where the rebels wanted to promote Protestantism, hence their demands for improved clerical standards. However, the moderate Elizabethan Settlement helped end religious unrest and confine it to the middle of the period.

The response shows clearly how religion was a cause for only part of the period. There is evidence of continuity with evidence that the aims were to restore Catholic practices. However, the awareness of subtlety is there with Kett. Strong analysis continues to be a feature.

During the period dynastic and factional rebellions were ever present, but the former declined in severity, whereas factional unrest remained. However, there were also changes to the causes of unrest; taxation declined from a major cause under Henry VII to a subsidiary cause by the mid-Tudor period. Economic and religious causes emerged only in the middle and later period, but whilst economic causes remained for the rest of the century, religious rebellions disappeared after 1569. However, as most rebellions were multi-causal, there were elements of economic and social grievances in earlier rebellions, suggesting that the major causes of rebellion were present, with the exception of religion, throughout the period, but what changed was their relative importance.

The conclusion reinforces the opening argument, but there is also some modification. It shows that a well-argued response will not simply repeat the opening in the conclusion.

The essay contains relevant and accurate knowledge, which is used to drive the argument forward. It is clearly structured and the argument is coherent and easy to follow. The answer does focus on change and continuity and relates the material back to the question set. There is evidence of synthesis in all paragraphs and this ensures that the answer will reach the higher levels.

2 The frequency and nature of the disturbances

Location

> For a description of all the rebellions mentioned see pages 8–9.

Most rebellions took place in **peripheral** regions of the kingdom in part because they were furthest away from central government in London and the king was more dependent upon local nobles and gentry to maintain order.

The north

At the start of the period the north was a **Yorkist** stronghold as it had been Richard III's seat of power. Lovell and Stafford attempted to raise forces there in 1486. The 1489 tax rebellion had some Yorkist links, but was also the result of the region's **particularism** in not paying taxes, except to defend the Scottish border. The Pilgrimage of Grace in 1536–37 and Northern Earls in 1569 were in part a response to resentment at the growing power of London and the region's exclusion from decision making. The northern nobles felt their status had been undermined.

The south-west

The south-west was not concerned about dynastic issues, but resented the increased role of central government, particularly with regards to taxation. Cultural and linguistic differences, particularly in Cornwall, may have given the region a sense of difference and encouraged resistance to taxation and religious innovation.

East Anglia

There was a tradition of unrest in East Anglia, with outbreaks in 1381 during the **Peasants' Revolt**, **enclosure** riots in 1525 and attacks on the gentry in 1540, before the major uprising in 1549. The rebels established a series of camps in places where local government was administered, such as Bury St Edmunds.

Ireland

The distance from London and the difficulty of sending troops encouraged unrest. This grew as the period progressed because the government increased its control over the region – challenging the traditional **clan** power of families such as Tyrone, O'Neill and **Fitzgerald**. The attempt under Elizabeth to introduce Protestantism and the **plantation system** caused further problems.

Major towns and cities

In many of the disturbances the rebels attempted to seize the capital or the regional or religious centre. The Cornish (1497) and Wyatt (1554) rebellions both marched to London, whilst Essex attempted his rising there in 1601. The Pilgrims seized York, the regional capital of the north in October 1536, whilst Lincoln, the seat of the local bishop, had been taken earlier in the month. Similarly, the Northern Earls entered the religious centre of Durham to restore mass in 1569. In 1549, Kett's rebels seized Norwich, the regional capital of East Anglia, and the Western Rebels besieged Exeter, the regional capital of the south-west, although they failed to take it.

Tradition

Some rebels focused on sites of earlier unrest. The Cornish went to Blackheath in June 1497, where the Peasants' Revolt had gathered in 1381. The Western Rebellion, 1549, started at Bodmin, as had the Cornish rising of 1497. The Oxfordshire rising of 1596 gathered at Enslow Hill, which had been the site of a gathering in 1549.

The importance of the nobility

Areas were more likely to witness unrest if the relationship between the nobility and inhabitants was poor. This was seen in 1549 in the West Country where Lord John Russell had newly replaced the Courtenays, and in East Anglia where the Howards had fallen from power. Where control was strong, unrest was limited, for example in Sussex where the Earl of Arundel ruled.

Develop the detail

Below are a sample exam question and paragraph written in answer to this question. The paragraph contains a limited amount of detail. Annotate the paragraph to add additional detail to the answer.

'Rebellions always attempted to seize regional capitals.' Assess this view.

Many rebellions throughout the period attempted to seize regional capitals. Regional capitals were administrative centres and their seizure presented a direct challenge to the government who would have to send in troops to regain control as happened in 1549. Regional capitals were often the seats of the local bishops and in religious protests the rebels wanted to control these. However, they were not always successful in taking them, even when they laid siege to them. It was not just regional capitals that the rebels attempted to seize, many rebellions attempted to take the capital city itself because it was the centre of government. The situation in Ireland was very different as the rebel tactics were not the same and the seizure of major towns or cities did not occur.

Introducing an argument

Read the following sample exam question, a list of key points to be made in the essay, and a simple introduction and conclusion for the essay. Rewrite the introduction and the conclusion in order to develop an argument.

'Rebellion was more frequent in regions furthest from London.' How far do you agree with this view?

Key points:
- The regions which are furthest from London: Ireland, the north and west
- Unrest in London and East Anglia
- Nature of rebellion and distance from London
- Pattern of change over time?
- Policies in the peripheral regions

Introduction:

To an extent rebellion was more frequent in the regions furthest away from London. The regions furthest from London were accustomed to greater freedom and often saw themselves as almost independent, particularly during the early period when particularism and regionalism was very strong. However, unrest in London and East Anglia was also quite common.

Conclusion:

Rebellion was to some extent more frequent in the peripheral areas. Despite government policies, rebellion remained a constant threat. However, there were other areas, such as London, that saw unrest in the final years of Elizabeth's reign.

The size, frequency and duration

For a description of all the rebellions mentioned see pages 8–9.

Size of rebellions

The size of rebellions varied greatly, ranging from just four people in the Oxfordshire rising (1596) to around 40,000 in the Pilgrimage of Grace (1536–37). After the crisis of 1549, when perhaps 15,000 rebels entered Norwich under Kett, the numbers declined (see table below).

Date	Rebellion	Numbers
1497	Cornish	15,000
1525	Amicable Grant	10,000
1536	Pilgrimage of Grace	40,000
1549	Kett	15,000
1554	Wyatt	5,000
1569	Northern Earls	5,000
1601	Essex	300

This decline was perhaps a result of the failure of rebellions or because the social groups that often led rebellions were incorporated into the state through offices such as Poor Law administrators. This meant that later rebellions were usually led by nobles who were either impoverished or excluded and felt they had nothing to lose. These rebellions were also more often about 'high politics' that did not rouse popular support.

Numbers involved in Irish rebellions were usually small, but Tyrone's rebellion was the exception as he was able to raise 6000.

Frequency

There were two periods when rebellion was most frequent:

1 Under Henry VII, because he was insecure and had gained the throne by force. There were alternative claimants and foreign powers were willing to support them. Henry needed money to defeat the threats and raised taxes, causing further unrest.

2 The mid-Tudor period, 1536–54, because the crown was weak due to religious turmoil and rule by a minor and female. This coincided with a period of rising prices and social problems.

Under Elizabeth (1558–1603) the frequency of rebellions in England declined:

- The Tudors became more secure and removed rival claimants, such as the Poles, the leading Yorkist family with a claim to the throne. The Countess of Shrewsbury had been executed in 1541 by Henry VIII.
- The Elizabethan Church Settlement was moderate and helped to remove religious tensions that had caused unrest in the mid-Tudor period.
- Social and economic problems peaked in the 1540s and, although the 1590s were a time of economic hardship, government legislation, such as the Poor Law, helped to lessen the impact.
- The role of Justices of the Peace (JPs) and Lord Lieutenants was developed under Mary and Elizabeth; they helped to deal with issues at a local level.
- The gentry became less willing to lead rebellions and were incorporated into serving the state as JPs.
- Parliament and law courts were used more frequently to resolve disputes.

Duration

Although there appears to be no overall pattern to the duration of rebellions, a few points do emerge:

- Rebellions further away from London lasted longer because of the time taken to raise and send a force: Irish unrest often lasted years.
- Rebellions in the north and south-west lasted longer than other regions, for example the Cornish Rebellion lasted over a month, the Pilgrimage of Grace and the Western Rebellion over two months.
- Government underestimation of the seriousness resulted in rebellions taking longer to suppress. This was the case in Kett's rebellion of 1549.
- Rebellions near or in London lasted a short time as they threatened the seat of government. Consequently, the government raised troops quickly. For example, Wyatt's rebellion only lasted eighteen hours, and Essex (1601) was put down in twelve hours.

! Delete as applicable   a

Below are a sample exam question and a paragraph written in answer to this question. Read the paragraph and decide which of the possible options (in bold) is the most appropriate. Delete the least appropriate options and complete the paragraph by justifying your selection.

'1549 was the most important turning point in the nature of unrest in the period from 1485 to 1603.' How far do you agree?

To a **great/fair/limited** extent 1549 was the most important turning point in the nature of Tudor rebellions from 1485 to 1603. **Most/some/few** rebellions in the period before 1549 lasted a few months. This was particularly noticeable with the Pilgrimage of Grace which lasted two months and was similar to the major disturbances of Kett and the Western Rebellion in 1549. The Oxfordshire rising of 1596 and Essex rebellion in 1601 were **much longer/much shorter** in length. However, Irish rebellions, which became more frequent in the period after 1549, **support/challenge** this view as they sometimes lasted for a number of years. In this way, to a **great/fair/limited** extent 1549 was the most important turning point in the nature of Tudor rebellions from 1485 to 1603 because...

_____

_____

! Turning assertion into argument   a

Below are a sample question and a series of assertions. Read the exam question and then add a justification to each of the assertions to turn each one into an argument.

Assess the reasons why the frequency of rebellion declined in the period after 1550.

During the first half of the period the Tudor monarchy had been challenged by the Yorkists, but in the second half of the period this threat had been removed because...

_____

_____

During the period after 1536 religious changes had caused unrest but after 1559 this declined because...

_____

_____

Also the increased use of parliament meant that unrest was reduced because...

_____

_____

Leadership and support: Nobility

For a description of all the rebellions mentioned see pages 8–9.

Leadership and support

Leadership helped to determine the chances of success of an uprising and the threat it posed. Rebellions led by claimants to the throne or nobles were a threat to the monarchy. Although large-scale rebellions could present a challenge to the authorities, the nature of the support also affected the seriousness of the threat.

Royal claimants

Royal claimants made a rebellion more serious for the monarch, particularly when the monarch's legitimacy was dubious. Hence Simnel's claim to be Earl of Warwick (1486–87) and **Warbeck's** to be the Duke of York (1491–97) made Henry VII's position vulnerable because they had a stronger claim to the throne. However, Mary Tudor's legitimacy meant that the Duke of Northumberland was unlikely to succeed in 1553.

Nobility

Leadership by the nobility was particularly important in Ireland where nobles were heads of clans and could therefore mobilise large numbers. Noble leadership also helped to give the rebellion legitimacy and authority. The Cornish (1497) got Lord Audley to lead the tax protest and the Pilgrims (1536–37) besieged Pontefract Castle to persuade **Lord Darcy** to join. Sometimes nobles claimed they had been pressurised or threatened to lead the rebel armies, but given the likely punishments after defeat this claim was not surprising.

Although the nobility were supposed to be the monarch's agents in the localities, many rebellions attracted noble support. This was dangerous because they had finances, access to weapons and could gather their **tenants** to increase numbers involved.

Noble involvement was present throughout the period (see table below).

Date	Rebellion	Noble involvement
1486	Lovell and Stafford	Francis Viscount Lovell and Humphrey and Thomas Stafford
1497	Cornish	Lord Audley
1497	Warbeck	Lord Fitzwater, Sir William Stanley
1536–37	Pilgrimage of Grace	Lords Hussey, Darcy, Lumley and Latimer
1553	Northumberland's **coup** – **Lady Jane Grey**	Earl of Oxford, Earl of Huntingdon
1554	Wyatt	Duke of Suffolk
1569	Northern Earls	Earls of Northumberland and Westmorland
1601	Essex	Earls of Essex, Southampton, Sussex, Rutland and Lords Cromwell, Mounteagle, Sandes

It was Essex's rebellion which attracted most noble support. However, it should also be remembered that in most rebellions the monarch was also able to raise noble support. In the Northern Earls rebellion, Hunsdon, Huntingdon and Sussex were able to raise troops, the **Duke of Norfolk** was sent to stop the Pilgrimage of Grace and Mary Tudor was able to rely on most of the nobility to help her defeat Northumberland.

Support or challenge?

Below is a sample exam question which asks how far you agree with a specific statement. Below this is a series of general statements which are relevant to the question. Using information from earlier in the book, the opposite page and page 32, decide whether these statements support or challenge the statement in the question and tick the appropriate box.

'Rebellions led by members of the nobility were the most serious threat to the monarchy.' How far do you agree?

	Support	Challenge
Henry VII was forced into battle at East Stoke		
The Cornish rebels reached Blackheath		
Yorkist challenges remained throughout Henry VII's reign		
The protests against the Amicable Grant came from the peasantry		
The Pilgrims wanted Lord Darcy to lead the rising		
Robert Kett was a **yeoman**		
Robert Welch may have been the leader of the Western Rising		
Northumberland removed Mary Tudor		
Thomas Wyatt was a member of the Kentish gentry		
The Northern Earls raised only 5000 men		
Essex's rising lasted only twelve hours		

Complete the paragraph

Below are a sample exam question and a paragraph written in answer to this question. The paragraph lacks a clear point at the start but does contain supporting material and an explanatory link back to the question at the end. Complete the paragraph by writing in the key point at the start. Use the space provided.

'The nobility became less involved in rebellion as the period progressed.' How far do you agree with this view?

_____

_____

This point is supported by the fact that during the reign of Elizabeth individual nobles such as Westmorland, Northumberland and Essex led rebellions against the monarch. These nobles felt they were losing power and had little to lose; the Northern Earls had lost control of the wardenships of the Marches and Essex had lost his monopoly over sweet wine. Although they were able to attract support from some other nobles such as Southampton and Rutland, they were not able to attract popular support, with the Northern Earls raising only 5000 men. In comparison, the government was able to rely on the support of most of the nobility. In the Northern Earls rebellion, Hunsdon, Huntingdon and Sussex were able to raise troops, which forced the Northern Earls to flee and this can be contrasted with the Pilgrimage of Grace earlier in the period. Although there was something of change in the number of nobles involved in rebellion and the scale of those risings, the later period still witnessed noble unrest.

Leadership and support: Gentry and commons

For a description of all the rebellions mentioned see pages 8–9.

Leadership and support

Those in the gentry class or just below it, yeomen, often provided the leadership. They had organisational experience through holding local offices and were influential in local society.

The role of the gentry

As with the nobility, gentry leadership gave the rising some legitimacy. Gentry leadership became more common in the middle period, as nobles, unless they were seriously disaffected, were unwilling to risk their positions.

Date	Rebellion	Led by	Position
1489	Yorkshire Tax	Sir John Egremont	An illegitimate member of the Percy family
1536	Pilgrimage of Grace	Sir Robert Aske	Lawyer, attorney to the Earl of Northumberland
1549	Western Rebellion	Sir Humphrey Arundell, John Winslade and John Bury	They were all quite substantial landowners in either Cornwall or Devon
1554	Wyatt	Sir Thomas Wyatt, but also Sir James Croft and Sir Peter Carew	Wyatt was a courtier and former sheriff, Croft held a variety of government posts and Carew was a courtier and been High Sheriff of Devon and helped to put down the Western Rebellion

Clergy

Members of the clergy rarely led a revolt, as it was seen as a sin, but when the Catholic faith was under attack they did sometimes assume leadership roles. In the Pilgrimage of Grace the abbots of local monasteries were involved. In the Western Rebellion, some Cornish vicars marched to Exeter and the vicar of St Thomas Exeter, Robert Welch, may have been the leader of the rising. It was a priest, Richard Symonds, who first noticed Simnel's resemblance to Richard of York and initially encouraged the conspiracy.

Commoners

Few rebellions were led by commoners. They had little local influence and were unable to raise large-scale support, as was seen in Oxfordshire in 1596. However, the Amicable Grant rising in 1525 was led by commoners and was successful because they had sympathy in the King's Council. Much of the unrest in 1549 was led by commoners, particularly Kett in East Anglia, but also many of the lesser disturbances in the south and midlands.

Commoners were most likely to be involved in protests against government policies, notably taxation and religion (such as the Cornish rising of 1497 or the Pilgrimage of Grace in 1536). It was their involvement that ensured the rebellion raised large numbers.

Cross-class support

Some rebellions attracted support from across the whole social spectrum. This was seen in the Cornish rising, which was led by a noble, but attracted mass support, and in the Pilgrimage of Grace, which had support from all classes. However, some rebellions, such as Kett's, did not attract noble or gentry support because they were about low politics.

Foreign support

Foreign support was evident in the early dynastic rebellions, with Margaret of Burgundy funding mercenaries for Simnel's rebellion. Later rebels hoped to gain foreign support, but it never materialised:

- Pilgrimage of Grace (1536–37) – hoped for support from Charles V.
- Wyatt (1554) – hoped for support from France.
- Northern Earls (1569) – hoped for papal and Spanish support.

Simple essay style

Below is a sample exam question. Use your own knowledge, information on the opposite page and information from other sections of the book to produce a plan for this question. Choose four general points, and provide three pieces of specific information to support each general point. Once you have planned your essay, write the introduction and conclusion for the essay. The introduction should list the points to be discussed in the essay **and outline the line of argument you intend to take**. The conclusion should summarise the key points and justify which point was the most important.

> Assess the view that rebellions with cross-class support were the most threatening to the government in the period from 1485 to 1603.

 Identify an argument   **a**

Below are a series of definitions, a sample exam question and two sample paragraphs. One of the paragraphs achieves a high level because it contains an argument. The other achieves a lower level because it contains only description and assertion. Using information from earlier in the book and the opposite page, identify which is which. The mark scheme on page 7 will help you.

- **Description:** a detailed account.
- **Assertion:** a statement of fact or an opinion which is not supported by a reason.
- **Reason:** a statement that explains or justifies something.
- **Argument:** an assertion justified with a reason.

> 'The gentry were the most successful leaders of rebellion in the period from 1485 to 1603.' How far do you agree?

Sample 1:

> The gentry were involved in the leadership of a number of rebellions. Robert Aske, a Yorkshire lawyer, led the Pilgrimage of Grace and was able to get large numbers to rise up in support. He was also able to get the support of some important nobles such as Lords Hussey and Darcy. He was able to lead his troops to take York, the regional capital, and then seize Pontefract Castle. Therefore, Aske shows that gentry leadership was often successful.

Sample 2:

> There were occasions when gentry leadership was successful, at least in achieving some of the objectives of the rebellion. Robert Aske was able to raise a large force of 40,000 men which outnumbered royal forces and therefore seize the important city of York and the strategically important castle at Pontefract. Similarly, Thomas Wyatt was able to raise support from his local area around Maidstone, in Kent, and lead the rebel forces to the gates of the city of London before being defeated. Therefore, the rebellions led by the gentry were successful in achieving at least some of their initial objectives.

Objectives

> For a description of all the rebellions mentioned see pages 8–9.

The Tudor rebels usually had one of three main objectives:
- To remove the monarch (dynastic rebellions).
- To force the government to change its policies – such as taxation or religion.
- To remove English rule from Ireland and establish independence (Irish rebellions).

Dynastic rebellions

At the start of the period it was clear that the Yorkist rebellions of 1486, 1487 and 1497 had the objective of removing Henry VII from the throne. The removal of the monarch was also evident in the plot surrounding the 'Devise' in 1553, when Northumberland wanted to prevent Mary Tudor from acceding to the throne. However, other dynastic rebellions were less open in their objectives and often claimed that their aim was not to remove the monarch. This was certainly the case with:
- Wyatt (1554), who claimed he wanted to stop Mary's marriage to Philip
- the Northern Earls (1569), who wanted to force Elizabeth to name Mary Queen of Scots as heir
- Essex (1601), who wanted to remove the **Cecil faction**.

However, the aims of these last three rebellions may have concealed an ultimate aim to overthrow the monarch.

Change in government policies

Many of the rebellions were protests against government policies, particularly taxation and religious change.

Taxation

Tax rebellions often followed innovative practices, such as the introduction of taxes to fund wars, as in 1489, 1497 and 1525. The rebels wanted the government to stop the collection of the taxes.

Religious policies

Protests about religious changes usually followed legislation that had a significant impact on the daily lives of people. The Pilgrimage of Grace (1536–37) followed the dissolution of the smaller monasteries, which the rebels wanted reversed as well as demanding the restoration of traditional practices and papal rule. The Western Rebellion (1549) followed the dissolution of the **chantries** and the introduction of a new, Protestant, **Prayer Book**. The rebels saw this as an attack on traditional religion and wanted the changes reversed. Similarly, the rebels in 1569 wanted an end to the religious changes introduced by Elizabeth and her bishop in Durham, Pilkington.

Social and economic policies

There were also protests about social and economic policies. Kett's rebels (1549) wanted the government to enforce **anti-enclosure legislation** and protect **common land**. The Western Rebels (1549) wanted the government to abandon the **Sheep and Cloth tax**. In the Oxfordshire rising of 1596, it is likely the rebels wanted the government to take action against high food prices.

Ireland

At first, Irish rebellions had similar objectives to some of the English rebellions; they wanted an end to recent government political, religious and economic policies. However, by the end of the period the Irish wanted to remove the English administration and, similar to the Northern Earls, also preserve the Catholic faith.

Spot the mistake · a

Below are a sample exam question and a paragraph written in answer to this question. Why does this paragraph not get into Level 5? Once you have identified the mistake, rewrite the paragraph so that it displays the qualities of Level 5. The mark scheme on page 7 will help you.

How far did the objectives of Tudor rebellions remain the same throughout the period?

The objectives of Tudor rebellions remained the same throughout the period. The rebels usually wanted the government to change its policies; this was particularly true of religiously motivated rebellions. The Pilgrims wanted the government to end the closure of the monasteries and restore the authority of the pope. In the Western Rebellion the rebels wanted a reversal of policy as they wanted the new Prayer Book abandoned, although there was no call for the restoration of the pope.

Eliminate irrelevance

Below are a sample exam question and a paragraph written in answer to this question. Read the paragraph and, using information from the page opposite and earlier in the book, identify parts of the paragraph that are not directly relevant to the question. Draw a line through the information that is irrelevant and justify your deletions in the margin.

'The reversal of government policies was the most common objective of Tudor rebellions in the period from 1485 to 1603.' How far do you agree?

Many Tudor rebellions wanted to reverse government policies. This was particularly true of religiously motivated rebellions where the rebels wanted to stop religious innovation, such as in the Pilgrimage of Grace where they wanted to preserve traditional religious practices, for example saints' days and holy days. This was similar in the Western Rebellion which was caused by the introduction of the new Prayer Book. Similarly, the rebels in the rebellion of the Northern Earls were concerned by the establishment of a Protestant regime in the north. However, in contrast Kett's rebels wanted to increase the moves towards Protestantism and wanted the government to ensure priests were resident and could teach the people.

Strategy, tactics and organisation

For a description of all the rebellions mentioned see pages 8–9.

Strategy and tactics

The strategy and tactics deployed by rebels depended upon their objectives.

Dynastic rebellions

Aiming to overthrow the monarch meant having to raise a large army, force the monarch into battle and have an alternative ruler available.

- Northumberland supported the claim of Lady Jane Grey (1553).
- Wyatt supported Elizabeth (1554).
- The Northern Earls supported Mary Queen of Scots (1569).
- Essex supported James VI of Scotland (1601).

Simnel (1486–87) and Warbeck (1491–97) landed in remote areas and hoped to gain support from disaffected counties as they marched towards London. However, both Wyatt's and Essex's rebellions began near London to try to seize the capital quickly.

Change in government policies

Rebellions where the objective was to pressurise the government into changing policies used a range of tactics. They:

- tried to raise as much support as possible, particularly the support of nobles and gentry who would bring their tenants with them; for example, the Pilgrims (1536) besieged Lord Darcy in his castle at Pontefract to get his support
- drew up a series of grievances containing their demands; for example, Pilgrims, Western (1549) and Kett's (1549) all drew up **articles**
- threatened or intimidated local gentry; for example:
  ○ the Pilgrims threatened Lord Darcy, Marmaduke Neville and Sir Roger Cholmeley
  ○ Western Rebels imprisoned gentry on St Michael's Mount
  ○ Kett's rebels imprisoned gentry such as Sir Roger Woodhouse, Thomas Gawdy and Richard Catlyn
- used violence; for example:
  ○ Yorkshire rebels (1489) murdered the Earl of Northumberland as he tried to collect taxes

○ William Hellyons was murdered by the Western Rebels who also shouted 'Kill the gentlemen'
- besieged regional capitals and county towns; for example:
  ○ the Cornish (1497) and Western Rebels besieged Exeter
  ○ Kett's rebels took Norwich
  ○ the Pilgrims entered York and Durham
  ○ Durham was entered again by the Northern Earls.

Irish rebellions

The rebels usually avoided military confrontation and conducted a campaign that was similar to modern **guerrilla warfare**. They attacked officials in order to try to disrupt government. If defeated they often disappeared into remote areas which the English forces did not know and would not enter.

Organisation

Organisation was vital in holding a rebellion together, but some rebellions were better organised than others. The following are the best examples of well-organised rebellions:

- The Pilgrimage of Grace – Aske was able to control 40,000 rebels from a range of social classes. The army was organised into '**hosts**' based on regions. The leaders of the hosts met to discuss tactics, pledging an oath, which helped ensure good discipline.
- Kett's rebellion – Kett controlled 16,000 rebels at the camp on Mousehold Heath. His aim was to show how local government could be run effectively. **Warrants** were issued for supplies, negotiations were undertaken with the Mayor of Norwich to buy supplies and prayers were said twice a day.

Poorly organised rebellions included the following:

- The Northern Earls rebellion – this was poorly planned as the earls had been reluctant to rebel. Moreover, their information gathering was poor as they were unaware Mary Queen of Scots had been moved south.
- Simnel's rebellion – his chances were lessened by the behaviour of the mercenaries who often pillaged and stole, which dissuaded locals from joining.
- Essex's rebellion – this lacked surprise as he gave notice of some action by having **Shakespeare's** *Richard II* performed the night before. The play culminates with the overthrow of Richard, suggesting the potential overthrow of the monarch.

! Delete as applicable

a

Below are a sample exam question and a paragraph written in answer to this question. Read the paragraph and decide which of the possible options (in bold) is the most appropriate. Delete the least appropriate options and complete the paragraph by justifying your selection.

Assess the view that Tudor rebellions were badly organised.

*Most/some/no Tudor rebellions were badly organised. For example, the leadership of the Northern Earls rebellion was similar to that of all rebellions to a **limited/fair/great** extent in that it lacked commitment from the rebels and was poorly informed. In contrast, Aske was similar to **all/some/few** of the other rebel leaders in ensuring that the Pilgrim rebels did not disperse and that order was maintained within the forces assembled. In Kett's rebellion he was able to exert a **limited/reasonable/considerable** degree of control through the issuing of warrants. In conclusion, the examples of the Northern Earls, Aske and Kett show that organisation of Tudor rebellions was **often/sometimes/never** poor in the sense that. . .*

_____

_____

↕ RAG – rate the timeline

Below are a sample exam question and a timeline. Using information from the opposite page and earlier in the book, read the question, study the timeline and, using three coloured pens, put a Red, Amber or Green star next to the events to show the following:

- **Red:** events and policies that have no relevance to the question.
- **Amber:** events and policies that have some significance to the question.
- **Green:** events and policies that are directly relevant to the question.

1 'Most Tudor rebellions wanted to avoid a battle with government forces.' How far do you agree?

Now repeat the activity with the following questions.

2 'The tactics of rebels in the period from 1485 to 1603 remained the same.' How far do you agree?

3 To what extent were Tudor rebellions poorly organised?

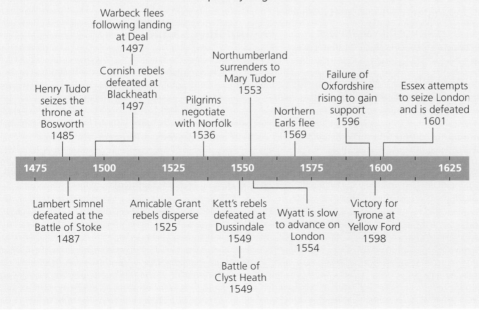

Differences between rebellions in England and Ireland

For a description of all the rebellions mentioned see pages 8–9.

Duration and scale

Irish rebellions usually lasted much longer than English rebellions. There were a number of reasons for this:

- The English government was reluctant to send large forces to Ireland because of the cost.
- They were seen as less threatening because of the distance from London.
- The rebels avoided open warfare and were therefore harder to defeat.

Unlike English rebellions, the scale of Irish unrest increased as the period progressed. This meant that English forces had to increase. **Sir Edward Poynings, Lord Deputy** under Henry VII, had 400 troops, but **Lord Mountjoy**, Deputy from 1600, needed 13,000 to defeat Tyrone (1595–1603).

Loyalty to the monarch

Most rebels claimed to be loyal to the monarch. However, Irish leaders were more likely to change sides and break truces.

- The **Earl of Kildare** backed Simnel (1486–87), then swore allegiance to Henry VII but failed to arrest Warbeck (1491–97) when he landed.
- The Earl of Desmond was held in the Tower of London for five years to try to win his support, but it only encouraged him to take part in the Geraldine rebellion of 1579.
- O'Neill had been brought up in the household of the Earl of Leicester and had helped with the defence of English garrisons between 1593–94, but because he was not rewarded he led the Tyrone rebellion. He signed a truce with the English in both 1596 and 1599, but used the time to build up forces to continue the rebellion.

Irish rebellions were more likely to end when the leaders were killed. However, this did not always happen as Desmond took on the leadership of the unrest after Fitzgerald's death in 1579.

Support

Unlike English rebellions, there were no popular rebellions in Ireland. All the rebellions were led by clan chiefs, who tried to get the support of their tenants in the same way as the Northern Earls. Unrest in Ireland was localised or regional and rebellion centred on the lands of the clan, except Tyrone's rebellion, which was nationwide.

Causes

Unlike English rebellions, Irish rebellions were not caused by social and economic problems. There were three major causes of Irish unrest:

- Imposition of direct rule from London.
- The growing influence of English families.
- Religious changes.

Imposition of direct rule

In Ireland, Henry VIII ended rule by the Irish nobility and declared himself king in 1541. This meant the clan chiefs had to surrender their lands and have them re-granted according to English laws and renounce their customs, language and laws. They saw this as an attack on their traditional way of life.

The growing influence of English families

In Ireland, after 1534, English officials were given administrative posts that had usually been given to Irish families. This lost the crown the support of families such as the Kildares. The problem was worsened by the **plantations system**, by which land was taken from rebels and granted to English landlords at reduced prices.

Religious changes

Although religion was a major cause of unrest in England between 1536 and 1569, in Ireland it was only a subsidiary cause or cloak, used to increase support. Clan chiefs often claimed that they were protecting the Catholic Church, but their primary concern was to protect their interests. However, the arrival of Catholic **missionary priests** after Elizabeth's **excommunication** in 1570 did encourage religious resistance and it can be seen as a feature of later rebellions.

Simple essay style

Below is a sample exam question. Use your own knowledge, information on the opposite page and information from other sections of the book to produce a plan for this question. Choose four general points, and provide three pieces of specific information to support each general point. Once you have planned your essay, write the introduction and conclusion for the essay. The introduction should list the points to be discussed in the essay **and outline the line of argument you intend to take**. The conclusion should summarise the key points and justify which point was the most important.

To what extent was the nature of English and Irish rebellions different?

Similarities and differences

Use the information on the opposite page and your own knowledge to complete the following table to show the similarities and differences between English and Irish rebellions.

Factor	Similarity	Difference
Geographical location		
Numbers involved		
Aims and objectives		
Leadership		
Tactics of rebels		

The success and failure of rebellions

> For a description of all the rebellions mentioned see pages 8–9.

Although most rebellions were defeated, often on the battlefield, with heavy casualties, as at East Stoke (1486), Clyst (1549) and Dussindale (1549), not all ended in failure. It is easy to see that those that aimed to overthrow a monarch were a failure, but harder to judge those that aimed to raise grievances. On some occasions the government did make concessions or introduce legislation to deal with the grievances.

The Amicable Grant Rising, 1525

This did achieve its aims as the tax was not collected and the parliamentary subsidy was also reassessed. It was a success because:

- it had considerable support, growing from 4000
- there was cross–class support
- there was resistance in London, which threatened the government
- Henry could make concessions without losing power
- Henry could blame Wolsey for the tax and by abandoning it improve his own reputation.

Demonstrations and concessions

The government made concessions in other taxation and social and economic rebellions. However, in most instances the government did not address the rebels' demands.

Date	Rebellion	Concession
1489	Yorkshire	The tax was not collected and rebels not fined
1497	Cornish	The tax was not collected, but rebels were fined
1536	Pilgrimage of Grace	The rebels were pardoned, but the parliament promised in the north was not called. Religious changes slowed down. Entry fines were set at the level demanded, the 1534 subsidy was stopped and Statute of Uses repealed
1549	Kett	Subsidy and Vagrancy Acts repealed. Enclosure Act restricts landlords' rights over common land. Acts fix grain prices and maintain arable land
1549	Western	Sheep and Cloth tax abandoned
1596	Oxfordshire	Seven landowners prosecuted for enclosing common land. Acts passed against decaying towns and to maintain arable land

Rebellions that were more successful:

- were usually taxation rebellions as the government was more willing to make concessions
- were well led, often by gentry, lawyers or yeomen
- had cross-class support.

Rebellions that failed

These were usually aimed at overthrowing the monarch or changing major government policies.

Dynastic rebellions

The government had to deal effectively with them to maintain its position; this was particularly true for Henry VII and Mary. Military action was often taken against dynastic threats, as with Simnel and Wyatt.

Religious rebellions

Rulers were unwilling to reverse religious changes because it would have shown weakness and encouraged further unrest. The concessions made after the Pilgrimage of Grace were only temporary and soon reversed.

- Henry VIII closed the larger monasteries in 1538.
- Edward VI did not abandon the Prayer Book in 1549 after the Western Rebellion.
- Mary did not abandon Catholic policies after Wyatt's rebellion.
- Elizabeth introduced penal laws against Catholic recusants after the Northern Earls in 1569.

Why did rebellions fail?

- Many lacked support or leadership from the gentry or yeomen and this meant they lacked adequate leadership.
- Government tactics, such as pardons, encouraged some to disperse. The government played for time so rebel supplies ran out, they needed to return for the harvest or divisions developed.
- The threat of a royal army caused some to desert.
- The government forces were superior and defeated the rebels every time. The government could also call on foreign mercenaries, as in 1549.
- Many rebellions were about local issues and therefore did not attract widespread support. Kett's rebellion was about grievances in East Anglia and the Cornish was about tax in the county.
- The rebels failed to capture London. When the rebels reached London the government acted quickly, the Cornish were slaughtered at Blackheath, the gates were closed on Wyatt and Essex was met with force.
- Foreign aid either failed to arrive, as in the Northern Earls, or was too small, as with Simnel.

Support or challenge?

Below is a sample exam question which asks how far you agree with a specific statement. Below this is a series of general statements which are relevant to the question. Using your own knowledge, the information on the opposite page and earlier in the book, decide whether these statements support or challenge the statement in the question and tick the appropriate box.

'Rebellions under Henry VII and Henry VIII were more successful than those after 1547.' How far do you agree?

	Support	Challenge
Simnel fought Henry VII at the Battle of Stoke		
The Yorkshire tax rebels were not punished and the tax was not collected		
The Cornish did not have to pay the war tax in 1497 but were heavily fined		
Warbeck's attempted landings were a failure		
Henry had to abandon his French campaign because of the failure to raise the Amicable Grant		
The Dissolution of the Monasteries was speeded up after the Pilgrimage of Grace		
Social and economic reforms were introduced after the 1549 unrest		
Mary Tudor was able to regain the throne		
Wyatt was able to reach the gates of the city of London		
The Oxfordshire rebels were executed		
Essex's rebellion was defeated in twelve hours		

 Introducing an argument

Read the following sample exam question, a list of key points to be made in the essay, and a simple introduction and conclusion for the essay. Using the information on the opposite page and earlier in the book, rewrite the introduction and the conclusion in order to develop an argument.

'All Tudor rebellions ended in failure.' To what extent do you agree with this view?

Key points:

- The measurement of failure
- Causes of the rebellion – dynastic, tax, religious, social, factional
- Nature of the rebellion – protest?
- Government policies – legislation after the unrest
- The results of rebellion – retribution

Introduction

To an extent all Tudor rebellions ended in failure. The rebels were not able to change the monarch or government policies in most instances. Most rebellions ended with the deaths of the rebels. However, in some instances, the rebels were able to raise large forces and mount a challenge to the government.

Conclusion

Rebellions were both a success and a failure. They often failed to achieve their ultimate aim of removing the monarch or changing the religious policies. However, there were other ways in which they were a success; many raised large numbers or forced the government to introduce legislation to deal with their grievances. Therefore, Tudor rebellions were both a success and failure.

Exam focus

Below is a sample of a high-level essay in response to an exam-style question. Read the essay and the comments around it.

To what extent did Tudor rebellions in England fail to achieve any of their aims?

Throughout the period 1485–1603 Tudor rebellions largely failed to achieve any of their aims whether dynastic, economic or religious. However, the success in bringing about the abandonment of the Amicable Grant in 1525 and the piecemeal successes made by the Lincolnshire rebels and the Pilgrims in 1536 in slowing down the abandonment of some Catholic practices shows that not all Tudor rebellions failed to achieve their aims; but in the main rebellion still ended in defeat.

Dynastic rebellions throughout the period failed in the main to achieve their aims. However, the success of Henry VII at Bosworth in 1485 and the limited success of Lady Jane Grey through Northumberland's coup of 1553 show that not all Tudor rebellions were complete failures. The Yorkist monarchy was successfully toppled in 1485 and the succession of Mary was successfully challenged in 1553, albeit for only nine days. However, in the main dynastic rebellions, such as Lovell and Stafford in 1486, Simnel and Warbeck failed to achieve any of their aims. This was because of the royal army at Stoke, but in the 1490s, when Warbeck was successfully driven from Ireland and England, it was the lack of support from either foreign mercenaries or nobility which condemned the rising to failure.

Economic rebellions throughout the period 1536–96 achieved some limited successes in fulfilling their aims. The Western Rebels of 1549 successfully managed to prevent the levying of the unpopular Sheep and Cloth tax. However, neither the Western or Kett's rebels were able to end enclosure or the loss of common land. Similarly, in 1596, the Oxfordshire rebels were unable to halt the progress of enclosure. Despite this, the demands of the Pilgrims in 1536 and Kett's rebels to reduce entry fines and improve wages were partially met, although the issue of wages was only resolved in 1563 with the Statute of Artificers, which fixed maximum not minimum wages, hardly a direct result of the unrest. However, in most instances the lack of cross-class support for low politics and economic rebellions meant that they largely failed to achieve their aims and at best made piecemeal gains.

Taxation rebellions were the most successful of all Tudor rebellions, with most achieving at least some success and making some limited gains throughout the period 1489–1549. The Yorkshire and Cornish tax rebellions of 1489 and 1497 both achieved their aims as they successfully avoided paying the taxes designed to fund wars in France and Scotland respectively. However, despite this success the Cornish rebels suffered a crushing military defeat at Blackheath and this was coupled with economic sanctions that were imposed on the area after their defeat. The Amicable Grant unrest of 1525, unlike either 1489 or 1497, was a complete success; as well as the tax not being collected, which was the main aim of the rebels, the aftermath of the rebellion, unlike 1497, resulted in no slaughter of the rebels, just the abandonment of the tax. Similar success can be seen with the Sheep Tax of 1549, which, like the rebels in the Amicable Grant unrest in 1525, the rebels were able to stop.

A clear view about the issue in the question is offered, but the response is aware of some variations to this. The thesis is clear and it will allow the examiner to read the final paragraph and decide whether this has been shown.

The opening sentence links back to the question. There is some evidence of continuity and synthesis, shown through the final section on the defeat of dynastic unrest under Henry VII.

The opening sentence offers a clear view. There is some evidence of synthesis in a balanced discussion, with the candidate suggesting that some of the gains were not due to rebellion.

A clear view that taxation rebellions were the most successful is offered. This argument is supported with precise details and shows synthesis across the period where taxation was an issue. However, there is no comparison with other rebellions to show that taxation rebellions were the most successful and this will impact on the final mark.

Quick quizzes at **www.hoddereducation.co.uk/myrevisionnotes**

Factional rebellions were present throughout the period but had very limited success. Both the Amicable Grant and the Pilgrimage of Grace, which hoped to remove the king's ministers, Wolsey and Cromwell, may have succeeded in planting seeds of discontent in Henry's mind – Wolsey fell five years after the Amicable Grant and Cromwell fell four years after the Pilgrimage of Grace – but did not achieve immediate success and their falls cannot be directly linked to the unrest. Both the Northern Earls and Essex's rebellions, which aimed to remove the Cecil faction, failed as the family dominated politics throughout Elizabeth's reign. Perhaps the overthrow of Somerset by Northumberland can be seen as the only successful factional incident as throughout the period those in favour were able to maintain the support of the monarch and therefore defeat their challengers.

> Again there is a clear line of argument. Continuity and synthesis is shown, although a concluding sentence pulling the paragraph together would have helped.

Religious rebellions in the period 1536 to 1569 had little success in achieving their aims. Religious rebellions attempted to reverse the religious changes that the government had implemented. The Pilgrimage of Grace may have speeded up the process of dissolution, encouraging full suppression in 1539. However, the rebellion might also have encouraged Henry to adopt a more conservative approach, with the Six Articles, but this gain was insignificant when compared with their demands to restore Catholicism to the position of pre-1529. Compared to this limited success, the Western Rebels and Northern Earls achieved even less. The Western Rebels' protest against the moderate Prayer Book led to an even more Protestant Second Prayer Book in 1552, whilst the Northern Earls saw no restoration of Catholic practices and instead the full implementation of the Elizabethan Church Settlement and the increased Protestantisation of the north.

> There is a synoptic approach and the response analyses the argument before reaching a conclusion, showing similarity between all religiously motivated unrest.

Overall, throughout the Tudor period not all rebellions failed to achieve any of their aims; however, only the Amicable Grant rebellion was completely successful. Some rebellions did achieve some of their subsidiary aims, such as the Western over the Sheep Tax, or were successful in the short term, as with Lady Jane Grey. Some economic grievances were addressed, as in 1536 and 1549, but both sets of rebels failed to achieve their main aims of reversing religious changes. Even with economic rebellions, the main concerns were not really addressed until the 1590s, when, faced with serious food shortages, Elizabeth's government introduced a range of measures to ameliorate the situation. Religious rebellions failed to prevent the implementation of government policy. As a result, it was only taxation rebellions, notably those of 1489, 1497 and 1525, which achieved their main aims, suggesting that, although most failed to achieve their aims, not all did.

> The conclusion does slightly modify the opening paragraph but does not deviate significantly from the original thesis. The response makes a valid point that when some aims were achieved they were often subsidiary, but this could have been developed in the main body of the essay.

Although the essay shows a good understanding of continuity and change across the period and supports the arguments with relevant and accurate material, some paragraphs lack the developed judgements needed for the highest levels. There is good explanation and analysis of the topic, but in places it is uneven, as in the paragraphs on taxation and faction. The answer does remain focused on the question set and there is evidence of synthesis throughout.

Exam focus activity

Use the comments and the mark scheme on page 7 to make a list of additional features that would enable this answer to reach full marks. In particular, look at the opening paragraph. Remember that an answer receiving full marks is not a perfect answer, but one that is 'best fit' with the level descriptors in the mark scheme.

3 The impact of disturbances on Tudor governments

Government strategy: Initial responses

> For a description of all the rebellions mentioned see pages 8–9.

Consultation

Tudor monarchs either consulted with their councillors or left their councillors and secretaries to deal with the unrest, but insisted on being kept informed.

- Henry VII consulted with **household servants** and called a **Great Council** when Simnel invaded in 1486.
- Henry VIII left **Wolsey** and **Cromwell** to deal with the rebellions.
- Mary and Elizabeth relied on their secretaries and councillors to devise strategy.

The exception to this was the **Duke of Somerset** who, whilst acting as Protector for Edward VI, was criticised for failing to consult the **Privy Council** when rebellion broke out in 1549.

Sometimes monarchs received conflicting advice. During Wyatt's rebellion in 1554 some councillors suggested using imperial troops to put down the rising and others suggested Mary should leave London. However, it was her decision to stay that defeated the rising as her speech to the crowds in London rallied support to her.

Gathering information

It was important for the monarch to obtain accurate information about the nature and scale of rebellions. This was often a slow process as communication with the **peripheral** regions was difficult, so sometimes the monarch was inactive or made the wrong decisions. Throughout the period the monarchs used spies, secret agents and informers to gather information about unrest.

- Henry VII used agents to follow the Staffords and Lovell (1486). As a result, the Staffords were arrested and Lovell was forced to flee.
- Henry VII had spies in European courts which kept him informed of the movements of **Warbeck** (1491–97).
- Elizabeth (1558–1603) used Francis Walsingham to keep her informed of potential unrest, particularly with regard to Mary Queen of Scots. He employed over 50 agents and their success is a factor in the decline of unrest after 1570.

However, there were times when this system failed.

- When Henry VIII ordered the Earl of Derby to arrest the leaders of the Pilgrimage of Grace he was unaware the earl was some distance from the rebels so could not carry out his orders.
- The Duke of Somerset was unaware of the failure of **Justices of the Peace (JPs)** to carry out his order to persuade the Western Rebels to disperse and the rebellion was able to grow in size. Ultimately a royal army had to be sent.

Government instructions

The first people expected to deal with the outbreak of unrest were JPs and **sheriffs**. If this failed, the nobility who lived in the area were instructed to restore order. The JPs and nobility met with varying degrees of success.

The Amicable Grant Rising, 1525

When the protestors threatened to march on London, the Dukes of Norfolk and Suffolk took command and successfully ended the unrest.

The Western Rebellion, 1549

The JPs were not strong enough to contain the rebellion. The government sent Sir Peter Carew, but his attitude inflamed the situation and turned a local protest into a serious rebellion.

Kett's rebellion, 1549

The failure of the **gentry** and sheriff to deal with the unrest resulted in the sending of the **Lord Lieutenant**, but he did not have enough troops and was defeated. As a result, the Duke of Northumberland was sent with reinforcements.

The Oxfordshire rising, 1596

The **Privy Council** had already warned JPs of the potential for unrest because of the food shortages. Informers warned the JPs of a plot and they were able to arrest the leaders before unrest broke out.

Develop the detail · a

Below are a sample exam question and paragraph written in answer to this question. The paragraph contains a limited amount of detail. Annotate the paragraph to add additional detail to the answer.

'The government was always slow in responding to the outbreak of rebellion.' How far do you agree?

When the government discovered that there was trouble, talks were often held between the monarch and councillors to decide what action to take and this could delay their response to the unrest. Henry VII consulted his trusted servants or called a meeting of nobles to decide what to do; this was different to Elizabeth and Mary. Henry VIII also left similar problems for his ministers to deal with. Somerset on the other hand adopted a different approach. Consultation and information gathering were lengthy processes, as the government wanted to know all the details about the unrest in order to decide what action to take. There were often delays in gathering information and this made the government appear slow.

Turning assertion into argument · a

Below are a sample exam question and a series of assertions. Read the exam question and then add a justification to each of the assertions to turn it into an argument.

To what extent was gathering reliable information the most serious problem for the government when dealing with the outbreak of unrest?

Some Tudor governments had problems gathering information because...

_____

_____

However, Henry VII's use of spies was successful as...

_____

_____

Also the significant use of spies under Elizabeth helped as it...

_____

_____

Government tactics

The government did not have a **standing army** or police force, and often with little money and other challenges had to use a range of responses to unrest.

Buying time

The government often threatened rebels with punishment unless they dispersed, but this seldom worked. Wolsey tried this with the Amicable Grant and Cromwell with the Pilgrimage, but the size of the rebel force meant the government had to negotiate whilst trying to increase its own forces.

Propaganda

Most importantly, the government claimed the Tudors were the legitimate government and rebellion was a sin against God. Rebels were told they were acting against the natural order or **Great Chain of Being**. Cromwell used a team of writers to attack the Pilgrims, with Richard Morrison writing: 'A lamentation in which is showed what ruin and destruction cometh of seditious rebellion.' Edward's government also launched a propaganda campaign against the rebels in 1549. **Cranmer** wrote a **homily** on obedience and John Cheke wrote *The Hurt of Sedition*. Preachers were sent to the rebel camp at Norwich.

Pardons

The government issued pardons to rebels if they returned home and threatened serious punishment if they did not. However, the pardons usually exempted the ringleaders.

Pre-emptive action

When there was rumour of unrest action was often taken, seen most clearly during the reign of Henry VII. In dealing with Simnel:
- the clergy read a **papal bull** which **excommunicated** the rebels
- the real Earl of Warwick was paraded to show Simnel was an impostor.

In dealing with Warbeck:
- pressure was put on foreign powers not to support him
- Stanley was executed for supporting Warbeck.

Mary also took pre-emptive action to stop Wyatt's rebellion from developing and this forced other plotters to flee.

Force

Although costly, there were times when force had to be used. This was particularly true with dynastic challenges. However, it was a last resort, particularly in Ireland, because of the terrain, communications and fear it would increase hostility.

Raising troops was slow and this was another reason why the government often used delaying tactics. The government was also concerned about the cost and the danger troops could cause if they were not paid. The government also relied on the nobility and gentry for troops, but laws limited retainers so that they could not raise a force larger than the monarch.

There were often troop shortages, which added to the crown's problems:
- In 1497 the Cornish rebels had a larger force than Lord Daubeney.
- In the Pilgrimage of Grace, the rebels had 40,000 troops and Norfolk, who led royal forces, only 8000.
- In 1549 the government faced numerous rebellions whilst at war with France and Scotland. The Western Rebels numbered 6000, whilst Russell had just 300 men and, in Norfolk, the Marquis of Northampton had 1500 men, but Kett had 15,000.
- In 1554 Norfolk was old and did not inspire royal forces who deserted to join **Wyatt**.
- At the start of the Northern Earls, the Earl of Sussex, who commanded royal forces, had only 1000 men, but the earls had 5000.

On all occasions, except the Pilgrimage, the government was eventually able to raise a larger force, but it took time and explains why the government appeared slow to respond militarily at the outbreak of unrest.

Support or challenge?

Below is a sample exam question which asks how far you agree with a specific statement. Below this is a series of general statements which are relevant to the question. Using your own knowledge of the whole period and the information on the opposite page, decide whether these statements support or challenge the statement in the question and tick the appropriate box.

'Force was the most effective method of responding to rebellion in England.' How far do you agree?

	Support	Challenge
It took Henry VII six weeks to raise a force against Simnel		
The government was worried about the threat posed by its own forces		
The Cornish rebels outnumbered Sir Giles Daubeney		
The Pilgrim army outnumbered Henry VIII's five to one		
The Western Rebels initially had a larger force than the government		
Lord John Russell was eventually able to raise a larger force than the Western Rebels		
The Marquis of Northampton had fewer troops than Kett		
The commander of Mary's forces against Wyatt was unable to prevent troops from deserting		
The reliability of government forces at the start of the Northern Earls rebellion was doubtful		
Over time the government was usually able to raise a larger force than the rebels		
The gathering of royal forces was often slow because of other commitments		

 Introducing an argument

Read the following sample exam question, a list of key points to be made in the essay, and a simple introduction and conclusion for the essay. Rewrite the introduction and the conclusion in order to develop an argument.

How successful were government tactics in dealing with the outbreak of rebellion?

Key points:

- What would be success for the government?
- How successful was buying time?
- How successful was propaganda?
- Did the rebels disperse with the issuing of pardons?
- The success of pre-emptive measures

Introduction:

There were four key measures used by the government when rebellion broke out. The policies used included the buying of time, pardons, propaganda, promises and pre-emptive measures to deal with the rebels. The success of each measure varied.

Conclusion:

There were four key measures used by the government when rebellion broke out. The most successful policy was the use of pre-emptive measures. This was more successful than the other policies.

The fate of the rebels

Some rebellions ended in battle, such as the Cornish, Simnel, Western and Kett, but there were many occasions when battle was avoided, as with the Pilgrimage of Grace, Wyatt and the Northern Earls.

Military confrontation

The government wanted to avoid battle and killing its own subjects. However, when battle did occur the number of casualties were usually high:

- Up to 4000 of Simnel's **mercenaries** were killed.
- Over 1000 Cornish rebels were killed at Blackheath.
- Some 4000 of the Western Rebels were killed at Clyst and Sampford Courtenay.
- The battle at Dussindale killed 3000 of Kett's force.

Others were often captured and later faced punishment, with Norfolk taking 800 rebels after the Pilgrimage of Grace and the Earl of Warwick entering Norwich after Kett refused a pardon and hanging rebel prisoners.

Ireland

Ireland witnessed few full-scale battles, but there were skirmishes which often led to the death of the **clan** leader:

- Shane O' Neill was killed in 1567.
- **James Fitzgerald** was killed in the Geraldine rebellion.

There were also military defeats for Irish rebels with O'Neill's force defeated in **Ulster** in 1567 and Spanish troops were defeated in both 1580 and 1601 when aiding Irish rebels. However, the Irish rebels did defeat English forces at Yellow Ford in 1598.

Avoiding battle

A large number of rebellions avoided battle:

- Warbeck fled in 1496 rather than face Daubeney's army.
- Aske ordered the Pilgrims to avoid battle.
- The Duke of Northumberland backed away from battle with Mary when he lost support from the Privy Council.
- Wyatt surrendered.
- The Northern Earls avoided battle and fled, although the Earl of Northumberland was captured.
- Essex avoided a battle in London.

Trials and retribution

Punishments varied according to the monarch. Henry VII and Mary were quite lenient, perhaps because their position on the throne was weak. Henry VIII and Elizabeth were quite severe.

Henry VII

He used financial penalties, such as **bonds and recognisances**, to punish rebels as they weakened the nobles and increased his wealth and power. He was initially lenient towards Simnel and Warbeck, but both were later executed, accused of plotting.

Henry VIII

He promised pardons to the Pilgrims, but this was only because he was outnumbered. Following **Bigod's rising**, he went back on his word. The accused were tried without a jury and a verdict without appeal given. In Lancaster, the abbot of Whalley, four monks, four canons and nineteen others were executed. Forty-six were hanged for the Lincolnshire rising and 132 from the Pilgrimage and Bigod.

Edward VI

Somerset had been lenient towards the lower orders and this lost him support. Northumberland, to regain support, took harsh action. After the Western rising 100 rebels were hanged in Devon and Somerset and **martial law** imposed in Cornwall. The leading cleric, Robert Welch, was hanged from his church. After Kett's rebellion the ringleaders were executed and Kett tortured, tried and executed.

Mary Tudor

Although she burnt **heretics**, Mary wanted to win over people after Northumberland's attempted **coup** and did not treat rebels harshly. Initially few of Northumberland's rebels were executed and it was only with Wyatt's rebellion that Jane Grey and her husband were executed. Only 71 were executed after Wyatt's rebellion, whilst 600 were pardoned. Mary did not execute Elizabeth, despite rumours of her link to the rebellion.

Elizabeth I

Elizabeth treated all rebels harshly. After the Northern Earls, Northumberland was executed and 450 rebels hanged. With the Oxfordshire rising the five ringleaders were executed. Essex was executed after his rising and others were punished financially. In Ireland martial law was used.

! Complete the paragraph

Below are a sample exam question and a paragraph written in answer to this question. The paragraph contains a point and specific examples, but lacks a concluding explanatory link back to the question. Complete the paragraph, adding this link in the space provided.

To what extent were all Tudor monarchs harsh in their treatment of rebels?

Henry VII's treatment of rebels was similar to that of Mary Tudor. Although rebels who engaged in treasonous activities knew that the penalty was death, not all rebels were put to death. As a consequence, some potential rebels had bonds and recognisances imposed upon them. Mary Tudor was also lenient in her treatment of rebels after Wyatt's rebellion, pardoning over 600. However, Henry VIII, Edward VI and Elizabeth I were harsh in their treatment of rebels. After both the Pilgrimage of Grace in 1536 and the Western Rebellion of 1549 over 100 rebels were put to death, but after the rising of the Northern Earls in 1569 over 450 rebels were hanged and, even after the minor Oxfordshire rising of 1596, Elizabeth put all five ringleaders to death. It would therefore be fair to conclude that...

_____

_____

‡ Identify an argument

Below are a series of definitions, a sample exam question and two sample conclusions. One of the conclusions achieves a high level because it contains an argument. The other achieves a lower level because it contains only description and assertion. Using the information on the opposite page and earlier in the book, identify which is which. The mark scheme on page 7 will help you.

- **Description:** a detailed account.
- **Assertion:** a statement of fact or an opinion which is not supported by a reason.
- **Reason:** a statement that explains or justifies something.
- **Argument:** an assertion justified with a reason.

How far did the government behave consistently in its treatment of rebel armies?

Sample 1:

Throughout the period the government was consistent in its treatment of rebel forces. Although it tried to avoid confrontation, by offering pardons, as with Kett, or negotiating, as with the Pilgrims, it did engage in battle with rebel forces, particularly those who challenged the Tudor dynasty or who would not disperse. In such circumstances the government acted quite brutally and inflicted large numbers of casualties on the rebel forces: 4000 rebels were killed at Stoke in 1487 and similar numbers were also killed in 1549 in both the Western Rebellion and at Dussindale during Kett's rising. Therefore, although the government tried to avoid brutal conflict, it would, when necessary, take harsh action.

Sample 2:

When battles did occur the government inflicted heavy casualties on rebel forces. Henry VII killed some 4000 mercenaries and supporters of Simnel at Stoke in 1487 and the Cornish rebels also saw over 1000 killed at Blackheath. During the reign of Henry VIII large numbers were killed at the end of the Pilgrimage of Grace, following Bigod's rising. Large numbers were also killed in 1549 at Dussindale, during the suppression of Kett's rebellion and during the crushing of the Western Rebellion. Elizabeth I also killed large numbers of Dacre's army after the rising of the Northern Earls.

> For a description of all the rebellions mentioned see pages 8–9.

The impact on the crown

The Tudors defeated all dynastic rebellions. As the period progressed the crown became stronger: Henry VII acted cautiously towards many rebels because of his weak claim to the throne, but Elizabeth was able to take ruthless action.

The impact on crown servants

Crown servants were the target of many rebels:
- Cornish rebels (1497) attacked Archbishop **John Morton** and **Sir Reginald Bray**.
- The Amicable Grant rising (1525) attacked Cardinal Thomas Wolsey.
- The Pilgrimage of Grace (1536–37) attacked Thomas Cromwell, Thomas Cranmer and Richard Rich.
- The Northern Earls (1569) attacked William Cecil.
- Essex (1601) attacked Robert Cecil.

However, no minister fell directly as a result of rebellion, although Wolsey's position was weakened. Cromwell fell four years after the Pilgrimage of Grace, but it was largely due to the failure of the Cleves marriage, which was unpopular with Henry, and his advanced Protestant beliefs.

The only minister who fell directly due to rebellion was the **Duke of Somerset**. His fall was the result of policies that favoured the lower orders, such as the **Enclosure Commission**, and his failure to suppress quickly the unrest of 1549.

The impact on foreign policy

Throughout the period rebellion had an impact on foreign policy. It often forced a change in foreign policy as dealing with the unrest reduced the forces available to pursue foreign aims.

Henry VII, 1485–1509

The Yorkshire rising (1489) occurred as Henry prepared to go to war with France over their acquisition of Brittany. The king raised a force, but the rebels fled. It did not delay the war but was a distraction for Henry. The challenge of Warbeck (1491–97) affected Henry's relations with Burgundy, France and Scotland. Henry signed the **Treaty of Étaples** with France and the **Treaty of Ayton** with Scotland to prevent their support for **Pretenders** and he put a trade embargo on Burgundy. The Cornish Rebellion (1497) had an impact on preparations to attack Scotland as troops had to be diverted and this forced Henry to sign a truce with Scotland.

Henry VIII, 1509–47

Henry's reign witnessed the clearest impact of rebellion on foreign policy. The failure to raise the Amicable Grant forced Henry to abandon an invasion of France in 1525, at the very moment France was at its weakest following the capture of **Francis I** by the **Holy Roman Emperor**.

Edward VI, 1547–53

The 1549 unrest had a serious impact on foreign policy. England had gone to war against Scotland in 1542. Following victory at Solway Moss in 1542, and a further victory at Pinkie in 1547, it was decided to try to conquer Scotland through a **garrisoning policy**. However, this policy had to be abandoned as the troops were needed to put down the rebellions. Moreover, the unrest encouraged France to declare war on England in August 1549, at the very time troops were needed to crush unrest.

Mary, 1553–54

Wyatt's rebellion (1554) encouraged anti-Spanish feeling in England and damaged Anglo-Spanish relations. In the long term this may have been a contributory factor in encouraging Spain to aid Irish rebels against England (see page 48).

The impact on domestic policy

> The government did introduce some policy changes after rebellions and these are considered on pages 52–53.

! Spot the mistake

Below are a sample exam question and a paragraph written in answer to this question. Why does this paragraph not get into Level 5? Once you have identified the mistake, rewrite the paragraph so that it displays the qualities of at least Level 5. The mark scheme on page 7 will help you.

To what extent did Tudor rebellions affect foreign policy?

> Rebellions usually had a limited impact on Tudor foreign policy. The greatest impact was on Henry VII; he was forced to make peace with Scotland so that he could deal with the Cornish Rebellion. Henry VII also put a trade embargo on Burgundy to stop them giving support to Perkin Warbeck. Henry VII also signed the Treaty of Étaples with France so that they did not give support to Warbeck. Therefore, it can be seen that foreign policy was affected during the reign of Henry VII.

⚲ Spectrum of significance

Below are a sample exam question and a list of general points which could be used to answer the question. Use your own knowledge and the information on the opposite page to reach a judgement about the importance of these general points to the question posed. Write numbers on the spectrum below to indicate their relative importance. Having done this, write a brief justification of your placement, explaining why some of these factors are more important than others. The resulting diagram could form the basis of an essay plan.

'The most important impact of rebellions on Tudor governments was the overthrow of crown servants.' How far do you agree?

1 The overthrow of the Duke of Somerset 1549

2 The trade embargo with Burgundy

3 The Treaties of Ayton and Étaples

4 The fall of Cardinal Wolsey and Thomas Cromwell

5 The abandoning of the garrison policy in Scotland 1549

6 The abandonment of the invasion of France 1525

Least important ←——————————————————————→ Most important

The impact of rebellion on society

> For a description of all the rebellions mentioned see pages 8–9.

Government response to the immediate aftermath of rebellion was often harsh, but there was also some willingness to remedy the rebels' grievances.

Religious policy

Tudor governments did not abandon their religious policies as a result of unrest. It may even be argued that rebellion speeded up religious changes. The Northern Earls rebellion was followed by **penal laws** against Catholics who did not attend church.

Taxation

Policy was often modified. For example:
- taxes were not collected after either the Yorkshire (1489) or Cornish rising (1497)
- the Amicable Grant was abandoned at the end of May 1525.

Social and economic policies

Changes to social and economic policies were most noticeable after 1549 and in the 1590s because the government wanted to claim that the causes of unrest, particularly in 1549, were social and economic rather than religious, and that they were taking action to deal with the problems.

There was a concern after the 1549 unrest to restore order. This was done by the passing of an 'Act for the Punishment and Rising of the King's Subjects' and Lord Lieutenants were given control of **county levies**, improving their training and making them more efficient. This was followed by a series of measures designed to alleviate the social and economic problems as the government feared that rising prices and unemployment had fuelled the unrest:
- 1551: revaluation of the coinage – this helped to stop the fall in the purchasing power of the coinage and therefore helped to lessen the rise in prices that had made labourers worse off.
- 1552: limit on the conversion of **arable** to **pasture** – this discouraged **enclosure**, which had been a cause of unrest in 1549 as fewer labourers were needed.

- 1552: corn dealers were licensed – this helped to control the price of corn.
- 1552: systematic collection and disbursal of **alms** – this helped provide aid to those in poverty.
- 1552–55: measures to regulate the cloth industry – the cloth industry was a major employer and a lack of regulation had resulted in falling standards and a decline in sales causing unemployment.

Similar measures followed the unrest caused by food shortages and the Oxfordshire rising in 1596 (see page 44).

The impact on regions

The north

Rebellion gave the crown the opportunity to increase its control over the north and this can be seen after both the Pilgrimage of Grace (1536–37) and the Northern Earls rebellion (1569).

After the Pilgrimage of Grace:
- the **Council of the North** was reformed, with lesser gentry given roles, whilst Henry assumed overall responsibility for the Marcher lands
- lesser gentry were appointed under Henry VIII as deputy wardens of the borderlands
- **Justices of the Peace (JPs)** were changed and those who had shown sympathy with the rebels were removed
- Henry VIII visited York.

After the Northern Earls rebellion:
- men without local connections, such as the Earl of Huntingdon, were brought in to run the Council
- **magistrates** who had Catholic sympathies were purged and replaced with Protestants.

Ireland

Although rebellion in Ireland was caused by changes in policy, it also encouraged further change. Some of the major Irish families, such as the Geraldines and Kildares, were replaced by English officials. Land was redistributed, the beneficiaries being English settlers. Land was also taken from monasteries and bishops to pay for the cost of putting down the unrest.

Simple essay style

Below is a sample exam question. Use your own knowledge, information on the opposite page and information from other sections of the book to produce a plan for this question. Choose four general points, and provide three pieces of specific information to support each general point. Once you have planned your essay, write the introduction and conclusion for the essay. The introduction should list the points to be discussed in the essay **and outline the line of argument you intend to take**. The conclusion should summarise the key points and justify which point was the most important.

> 'The losses outweighed the gains.' Assess this view of the impact of Tudor rebellions on society.

 Develop the detail a

Below are a sample exam question and paragraph written in answer to this question. The paragraph contains a limited amount of detail. Annotate the paragraph to add additional detail to the answer.

> How far was royal authority strengthened as a result of rebellion?

Perhaps the most notable area where royal authority was strengthened in response to rebellion was in the peripheral counties of the north. The north was a dangerous area for the Tudors. This was clearly seen in the reigns of both Henry VIII and Elizabeth I, who took action to improve royal control after the Pilgrimage of Grace and the rebellion of the Northern Earls. The monarchs were concerned to bring in men who they could trust and remove those who were less reliable, even if they had not been involved in unrest, and this was done in a number of areas of local government. This often meant that men of a lower social status, who owed their power to the monarch, were brought in to replace those who had influence in the area. Some monarchs went even further and visited it, but this was not a regular feature.

For a description of all the rebellions mentioned see pages 8–9.

Factors that increased the threat of rebellions

The size and nature of support

If the number of rebels was larger than the government forces it increased the threat. This was the case, at least initially, with:

- the Cornish rising (1497)
- the Amicable Grant (1525)
- the Pilgrimage of Grace (1536–37)
- Kett's rebellion (1549)
- the Western Rebellion (1549)
- Northern Earls (1569).

The rebellion was more threatening if it acquired foreign and noble support. This was the case with:

- the Simnel rebellion (1486–87)
- Warbeck's rebellion (1491–97)
- the Pilgrimage of Grace (1536–37).

The threat was further increased if the rebels were able to force the king into battle, as happened with Simnel. This threat was greater as Henry VII had only just come to the throne and was uncertain of noble support. Sometimes foreign powers were able to supply mercenaries or soldiers to fight for the rebels.

The aim of the rebellion

Rebellions that aimed to overthrow the monarch were the most serious threat. Thus the following rebellions constituted a direct challenge to the Tudors:

- the Simnel rebellion (1486)
- Warbeck's rebellion (1490–97)
- **Lady Jane Grey** (1553)
- Wyatt's rebellion (1554)
- Northern Earls (1569)
- Essex (1601).

Location

Rebellions that were close to, entered or occurred within London were also a greater threat as that made it easier for the rebels to remove the government. However, London remained loyal throughout the period, even when rebels entered the city. For example, Mary was able to rally the city against Wyatt. The city had also supported her against the Duke of Northumberland's attempt to put Lady Jane Grey on the throne a year earlier.

Factors that lessened the threat of rebellions

Government tactics

In many instances, such as the Pilgrimage of Grace, the government offered concessions to the rebels, but had no intention of keeping them once the unrest had died down. However, many rebels believed that their grievances would be resolved. The offer of pardons that accompanied most rebellions encouraged some rebels to disperse, whilst propaganda may have weakened their cause. When the government was able to delay rebel activity, many rebels returned home to tend their crops.

Nature of the unrest

Most of the rebellions in the period were localised protests against local grievances or government policies. They had no intention of overthrowing the government, but wanted concessions or a change in policy. Sometimes, as with tax rebellions, the government was able to grant this, which lessened the threat.

Government support

Throughout the period the government was able to maintain the support of the majority of clergy and nobility. The clergy were used to preach against rebellion, whilst the lack of noble support deprived the rebels of legitimacy and leadership.

However, Irish rebellions were different and were a serious problem. The government lacked a large force in Ireland to crush the unrest. Irish nobles and clergy were often opposed to the government and the rebels had the advantage of knowing the land. Towards the end of the period the rebels were able to gain Spanish support. As a result, the rebellions were often lengthy and costly affairs, but even in Ireland the government emerged victorious.

RAG – rate the timeline

Below are a sample exam question and a timeline. Using the information on the opposite page and earlier in the book, read the question, study the timeline and, using three coloured pens, put a Red, Amber or Green star next to the events to show the following:

- **Red:** events and policies that have no relevance to the question.
- **Amber:** events and policies that have some significance to the question.
- **Green:** events and policies that are directly relevant to the question.

1   To what extent were dynastic rebellions a threat to Tudor governments?

Now repeat the activity with the following questions:

2   'Rebellions with foreign support were a great threat to Tudor governments.' How far do you agree?

3   To what extent were the rebellions in peripheral regions a serious threat to Tudor governments?

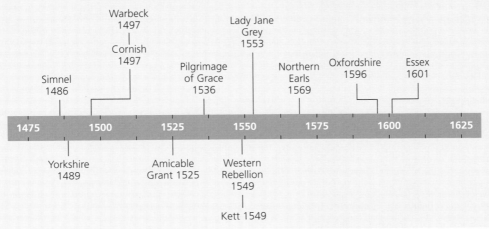

Turning assertion into argument

Below are a sample question and a series of assertions. Read the exam question and then add a justification to each of the assertions to turn it into an argument.

'Tudor governments were never seriously threatened by rebellion.' How far do you agree?

Rebellions were a threat to Tudor governments in so far as some rebellions were able to. . .

_____

_____

However, it was dynastic rebellions that were the greatest threat because. . .

_____

_____

Moreover, foreign support made these challenges greater because. . .

_____

_____

Exam focus

Below is a sample of a high-level essay in response to an exam-style question. Read the essay and the comments around it.

How effectively did Tudor governments deal with unrest?

During the period the frequency and severity of threat from rebellion declined, suggesting that as time progressed governments became more effective, particularly in England. Henry VII faced rebellions throughout his reign, with Warbeck's lasting for much of the 1490s, whereas Essex's rebellion in 1601 was defeated within a few hours. Numbers involved also declined; Essex raised only a few hundred and the Oxfordshire rising even fewer, whereas the Pilgrimage of Grace attracted 40,000, suggesting government became more effective. The poor economic conditions of the 1590s also failed to stimulate unrest, suggesting government legislation had been particularly effective in diminishing unrest. However, governments were less effective in dealing with Irish rebellions, which in the case of Tyrone's lasted for years.

> A clear line of argument is stated in the opening sentence, and this is briefly developed to suggest that in Ireland they were less effective. Some criteria against which effectiveness will be judged are suggested.

Without a standing army or a police force to maintain order, the government relied on the nobility and gentry to put down unrest in the localities. Not only did the government become more effective in winning noble support, but as the century progressed they won over the 'middling sort'. At the start of the period, Henry VII faced numerous rebellions which involved the nobility, with Stanley involved in the Warbeck conspiracy. However, through rewards and patronage the government was able to build up support so that in 1569 when the Northern Earls rebelled the Council of the North was able to put the rising down with relative ease. Similarly, Elizabeth had the support of nobles and the city of London to defeat Essex. Government reliance on the nobility was also effective in 1549; it was only in East Anglia and the West Country, where nobles were absent, that unrest developed into rebellion. However, in Sussex, Arundel was able to disperse rioters, suggesting that as the period progressed the reliance upon the nobility was largely effective.

> The response argues that the governments were effective in winning support for the regime. It shows evidence of change across the period and discussion of 1549 shows the importance of the nobility.

However, the government was not always effective, particularly at the start of the period when Henry VII was twice forced into battle at Stoke and Blackheath. Although victorious, battles were risky. Henry had seized the throne by force and the result at Stoke could easily have been reversed. Similarly, in 1549 government forces under Northampton were defeated at Norwich and Russell required five attempts to crush the Western Rebels. Military force was also ineffective in Ireland as the rebels often avoided full-scale military confrontation. Even after defeat in 1583, Tyrone, just a few years later, raised an even larger force which defeated the English, and it was not until Mountjoy's arrival that the rebellion was crushed.

> The theme of military action is considered. The response shows synthesis across the period, arguing it was not effective.

Negotiations and the offer of pardons varied in their effectiveness. Those protesting against the Amicable Grant dispersed and similarly Norfolk negotiated successfully with the Pilgrims, despite being outnumbered five to one. However, negotiation was not always successful. Neither Kett's rebels or the Western Rebels dispersed as a result of either pardons or negotiation. This forced the government to abandon its garrisoning policy in Scotland and commit large numbers of troops at the very time the country was under threat of invasion from France. Similarly, in Ireland, negotiations between O'Neill and the English commanders in both 1596 and 1599 failed to end the unrest.

> A further theme, negotiation, is discussed and although there is synthesis no judgement is reached.

Government strategy in dealing with rebellions became more effective as the period progressed. At the start, Henry VII sent troops to deal with the challenges of Simnel, the Yorkshire and Cornish risings and Warbeck. However, as the period progressed the policy changed and the government became more effective. Parliamentary legislation prevented unrest breaking out,

Quick quizzes at **www.hoddereducation.co.uk/myrevisionnotes**

particularly in the period after 1549. The effectiveness was most apparent in the 1590s, when, despite poor harvests and high grain prices, unrest was limited to the Oxfordshire rising. The issuing of Books of Orders to JPs and legislation on the movement of grain, along with the introduction of Poor Laws, all helped to dispel disquiet.

The greatest threat to Tudor rule came from dynastic challenges and the government was largely effective in removing this threat in England, but it was more difficult to eradicate in Ireland. Henry VII ultimately removed the Yorkist challenge, executing the Pretenders and Stafford, but was helped by the death of Lincoln and arrest of Suffolk. Similarly, the Courtenays were removed by Henry VIII, Mary Tudor destroyed the Greys and Elizabeth arrested and executed Mary Queen of Scots. However, in Ireland the situation was more difficult as Tyrone was able to raise a nationwide revolt against Elizabeth that lasted over eight years. Despite these challenges, a regime that had seized throne on the battlefield, with a limited claim, maintained the throne for over a hundred years.

The government's treatment of English rebels was usually effective, but their handling of Irish unrest suggests they had little understanding of their grievances. The seizure of lands, fines and destruction of property did not deter unrest and provoked further hatred which leaders, such as Desmond and Tyrone, were able to exploit. However, in England the government was more effective. Henry VIII was vindictive in his treatment of the Pilgrims and went back on his promise of pardon after the Bigod rising. However, this approach was largely effective as the northern counties were relatively quiet in 1549 and very few rose in support of the Northern Earls in 1569. Similarly, the numbers put to death by Edward VI's regime after 1549 was effective in discouraging later peasant unrest and may explain why so few joined Wyatt or rebelled under Elizabeth. When there was unrest under Elizabeth, as in Oxfordshire, the response was draconian – effective as the country remained quiet despite the poor economic conditions.

Most English disturbances were over quickly, suggesting the government was effective, with only the Pilgrimage, Western and Kett lasting more than a month. The strategies of propaganda, persuasion and threats usually maintained the support of the nobility and clergy and, by the end of the period, the gentry and 'middling sort'. The policy of 'buying time' was often effective and less dangerous or costly than military confrontation. However, once the government was in a strong position, reprisals against leaders was often effective in discouraging further unrest. It was only in Ireland that the government was less effective because the absence of permanent garrisons, the terrain and the increased unpopularity of government policies meant that it was difficult to maintain order, and this difficulty only increased as the period progressed.

> There is a clear line of argument in the first sentence and a synoptic approach is adopted. The paragraph would benefit from more precise examples.

> There is again a synoptic approach and a good comparison is made with Ireland. The paragraph also reaches a judgement.

> The thematic approach continues and there is a clear argument, with good analysis. Continuity and change across the period are shown.

> A valid conclusion is reached based on the argument in each paragraph. Even in the conclusion there is evidence of synthesis.

The answer remains focused on the question of 'how effectively' throughout and in most paragraphs reaches a valid judgement about the theme under discussion. The analysis is usually fully developed and the argument is well supported by appropriate and relevant examples. The answer also considers the question in terms of Ireland, an issue that is often ignored by many candidates.

Reaching judgements

In order to reach the very top level, candidates need to reach judgements about the theme they are considering in relation to the question. Identify the paragraphs where the candidate has successfully done this and those where a judgement is either absent or is not developed. In the latter cases write a couple of sentences for each of the paragraphs so that a judgement based on the argument is reached.

4 The maintenance of political stability

The role of the crown

For a description of all the rebellions mentioned see pages 8–9.

The importance of the monarchy

Although there was minor unrest and a significant number of rebellions, disorder was still the exception. When faced with challenges to its authority the government brought in short-term measures. Moreover, the monarchy was able to develop institutions and policies that resulted in the decline of rebellion. This section will look at the role of the central and local authorities in attempting to maintain stability.

The monarchy was the most important agent in the maintenance of stability. The monarch had ultimate authority, as they were appointed by God. Any rebellion against the monarch was seen as a sin against God. The monarch's authority was increased after the Reformation and Henry VIII's break with Rome, when subjects no longer held obedience to the pope in spiritual matters, only to God and the king.

The hierarchical nature of society reinforced the belief in obedience to the ruler. This was increasingly upheld through Tudor propaganda. Writers such as Richard Hooker and Edmund Dudley argued that everyone had a place in society and should accept it. The development of the printing press allowed such messages to be disseminated to a wide, increasingly literate, audience.

How did Tudor monarchs reinforce their authority?

- Office holders had to swear oaths of allegiance.
- Individuals and institutions swore **Oaths of Succession and Supremacy**.
- Monarchs issued proclamations which were read out in churches and market places.
- The use of propaganda.
- The use of **patronage**.

Propaganda

It is difficult to know how effective propaganda was, but all monarchs used it to a varying degree. Henry VII developed the image of the Tudor rose, which showed the unity of the Houses of York and Lancaster and claimed descent from the legendary King Arthur to bolster his claim to the throne. Henry VIII used paintings showing his physical presence and therefore his strength and power. This image was repeated on coins. He also built lavish palaces, such as Nonsuch, to reflect his authority. It was much harder for Edward, as a young boy, and Mary, as a female ruler who could not be shown in military dress, to portray their power. However, Edward's image did appear on coins and became more militaristic as his reign progressed, signifying his increasing authority and power. Yet it was Elizabeth who made the greatest use of propaganda. She toured much of southern and central England during many summers, undertaking **royal progresses** and staying with leading nobles and **gentry** so that she was seen by the people, reinforcing loyalty. **Pageants** were held frequently that depicted her as the instrument of stability and the saviour of the nation. Paintings were used to show her wisdom and leadership, particularly after the defeat of the **Armada**. She was also represented as Astraea, a mythical goddess renowned for her beauty, giving the impression that Elizabeth was her equivalent.

Patronage

All Tudor monarchs used rewards to keep the political elites subservient. Henry VII used the **Order of the Garter** (created by Edward III in the mid-fourteenth century) as the ultimate sign of honour by the king. Monarchs also used **peerages** and **knighthoods, grants of monopolies** and land to reward loyal servants. The possibility of gaining rewards attracted many to court and encouraged loyalty, providing the rewards were not dominated by one **faction**, as happened under Elizabeth when she bestowed numerous rewards on the Cecil family, sparking the Earl of Essex to rebel. Retaining the loyalty of the nobility was particularly important as the monarch had no army of their own and relied on nobles raising troops to put down unrest.

Identify an argument

Below are a series of definitions, a sample exam question and two sample conclusions. One of the conclusions achieves a high level because it contains an argument. The other achieves a lower level because it contains only description and assertion. Identify which is which. The mark scheme on page 7 will help you.

- **Description:** a detailed account.
- **Assertion:** a statement of fact or opinion, which is not supported by a reason.
- **Reason:** a statement that explains or justifies something.
- **Argument:** an assertion justified with a reason.

How far do you agree that all Tudor monarchs were successful in reinforcing their authority?

Sample 1:

Although all Tudor monarchs attempted to reinforce their authority, some were more successful than others. It was particularly difficult for Edward VI and Mary Tudor to accomplish this. However, the other monarchs were more successful and were able to use a variety of methods to achieve it. Royal authority was often reinforced by the use of propaganda and patronage. Monarchs went on progresses round the country and this helped to reinforce their image, as did the building of royal palaces or their portrayal in works of art. Tudor monarchs also gave out a variety of rewards, either titles or land, in order to keep the support of the nobility.

Sample 2:

Although all Tudor monarchs attempted to reinforce their authority, some were more successful than others. The most successful were Henry VIII and Elizabeth I, who not only made their subjects swear oaths to the Acts of Succession and Supremacy, but they also made use of both patronage and propaganda to maintain the loyalty of most of their subjects. Both monarchs rewarded loyal servants with grants of land and Elizabeth also issued grants of monopolies. They also ensured that they were portrayed as strong powerful rulers, either through paintings, as happened with Elizabeth after the Armada, or in military uniform for Henry VIII. However, Edward VI and Mary Tudor were less successful as neither of these monarchs could be portrayed in military splendour as Edward was a minor and Mary a female.

Turning assertion into argument

Below are a sample question and a series of assertions. Read the exam question and then add a justification to each of the assertions to turn each one into an argument.

'The institution of the monarchy was the most important element in the maintenance of stability.' How far do you agree?

The institution of the monarchy was important in the maintenance of political stability because...

_____

Moreover, monarchs worked hard to enhance their respect and aura because...

_____

However, they were also dependent upon the support of the nobility because...

_____

The role of the Church

For a description of all the rebellions mentioned see pages 8–9.

Throughout the period, the Church upheld the Tudor monarchy, even if some clergy and monks were involved in unrest. Despite the religious changes of the **Reformation** there was much continuity in the form of worship, the role of religion and even in parish clergy, which helped to create stability.

The Church had an important role in maintaining stability as it was a central influence in people's lives. It was usually the centre of the local community – carrying out baptisms, marriages and burials – as well as being the focus for most social life. Everyone was expected to attend church on Sundays. It also played an important role in supporting the crown in national life:

- Bishops were crown appointees, even before the Reformation.
- Bishops anointed monarchs with holy oil at the coronation.
- Clerics were used as advisors, for example William Warham and Richard Fox, who advised both Henry VII and VIII and Cuthbert Tunstall, **Thomas Wolsey** and Rowland Lee who advised Henry VIII. Henry VIII later appointed Lee to run the Council of Wales (see page 64). However, their importance did decline under Elizabeth.
- The Church leaders supported the crown against rebels; even the pope threatened with **excommunication** any who fought against Henry VII at Stoke, when Lambert Simnel had invaded, or Blackheath, when the Cornish rebels reached London.

The link with the state was strengthened after the Reformation as the Church came under the crown's **jurisdictional control** and bishops owed loyalty solely to the crown rather than the pope.

The parish clergy

The parish clergy played a vital role in local politics and had the power to both stabilise or destabilise the country. Attendance at church on Sunday meant that priests had the opportunity to instruct and remind people of their duties and obligations, or to encourage resistance. Clergy were encouraged to inform bishops of any rumours of trouble. The parish clergy also became important in the administration of the **Poor Law** and helped to control other social problems.

The Church and obedience

The Church could help to reinforce obedience through preaching, and sermons allowed the government to keep the country informed of its policies. In the 1530s priests were given detailed instructions on the content of their sermons and instructed to preach at least four times per year on obedience. Under Edward VI, **Thomas Cranmer** wrote a series of **homilies**, including one on obedience, which were read out during the unrest of 1549. In the 1590s bishops reminded their congregations of the government efforts to tackle social and economic problems.

Disobedience

Throughout the period the Church upheld order. However, there were times, particularly from 1530 to 1570, when the behaviour of some clergy appeared at odds with this objective.

Theories of disobedience developed during the sixteenth century when some writers argued it was God, rather than the monarch, who should be obeyed. Clergymen such as John Fisher, Hugh Latimer, Nicholas Ridley and Thomas Cranmer all adopted passive resistance: Fisher refused to acknowledge Henry VIII as Head of the Church and Latimer, Ridley and Cranmer refused to accept Mary's restoration of papal authority. These theories of resistance developed further under Mary's reign. Writers, such as John Ponet in 1556, argued that rulers had to be just and, if they acted against God, rebellion could be justified, provided it was led by a noble, **Justice of the Peace (JP)** or mayor. However, once the Protestant Elizabeth came to the throne these ideas declined among Protestants, although some Catholics took them up, supported by **papal sanction** after 1570.

Some clergy also encouraged social justice, with men such as Latimer arguing that obedience must be matched by the proper exercise of duty by those in authority.

Develop the detail

Below are a sample exam question and paragraph written in answer to this question. The paragraph contains a limited amount of detail. Annotate the paragraph to add additional detail to the answer.

'Throughout the Tudor period the Church consistently supported the crown.' How far do you agree?

> The Church was an important institution in the maintenance of stability. At the coronation of every monarch they were anointed with holy oil; a clear sign of the link between the Church and state. This link continued as many Tudor monarchs used bishops as administrators and for advice. Some monarchs appointed bishops to very high office, a clear sign of their dependence on them in the government of the kingdom. This process continued for much of the period, although the second half of the period saw less use made of bishops as administrators. The Church was also able to support the monarch by threatening or actually excommunicating any who fought against the king.

Introducing an argument

Read the following sample exam question, a list of key points to be made in the essay, and a simple introduction and conclusion for the essay. Using the information from the page opposite and from the rest of this section, rewrite the introduction and the conclusion in order to develop an argument.

How far did the Church help the maintenance of stability in England in the period from 1485 to 1603?

Key points:

To answer this question you should compare and contrast the impact on stability of the following institutions:

- The Church
- Parliament
- Nobility
- Lower orders
- The monarchy
- Royal councils
- Gentry

Introduction:

> To an extent the Church helped stabilise England in this period. The Church preached obedience to the monarch, with Cranmer writing a homily on obedience. The Church also threatened those who fought against Henry VII with excommunication. The break with Rome did not weaken the relationship between the Church and state as bishops were appointed by the crown and owed their loyalty to the monarch alone. During the later period monarchs did not use clergy as political office holders.

Conclusion:

> The Church was important in the maintenance of stability. Monarchs often looked to clerics for advice as with Henry VII and Henry VIII who used Bishops Fox, Warham and Wolsey, all of whom helped to administer the realm. However, the Church was not the only factor in the maintenance of stability and other institutions were more important.

The role of government policies

> For a description of all the rebellions mentioned see pages 8–9.

Although governments were frequently successful in dealing with political issues, the religious and economic policies, particularly in the first half of the sixteenth century, often caused unrest.

Religious policies

The religious reforms of Henry VIII and Edward VI were a cause of conflict. Henry VIII's dissolution of smaller monasteries was a cause of the Pilgrimage of Grace (1536–37). Edward VI's dissolution of the **chantries**, and the introduction of the 1549 **Prayer Book**, helped spark the Western Rebellion.

The **Elizabethan Church Settlement**, declaring her Supreme Governor and establishing a moderate Protestantism, was most effective in creating religious stability. She established outward conformity and most Catholics accepted the **Oaths of Supremacy and Uniformity**. The lack of support for the Northern Earls (1569) showed the policy's success.

Economic policies

Innovative taxation caused unrest in the early Tudor period (see page 12). However, after 1540 governments tried to find other ways of raising money to avoid heavy tax demands. They **debased the coinage**, sold crown lands, borrowed from overseas, cut expenditure and avoided war whenever possible. Most importantly, Elizabeth did not increase taxes in line with **inflation**. Therefore, unrest caused by financial policies declined.

Enclosure

The government was concerned to prevent enclosure as it caused unemployment. Commissions were established to enquire into unlawful enclosure and this encouraged people to use litigation, rather than force, to challenge enclosures. However, in 1548–49, the establishment of an Enclosure Commission under Protector Somerset provoked unrest as many believed that Somerset sympathised with their concerns. They believed that by throwing down illegal enclosures they were just enacting the Commission's likely findings.

Food supplies

Many of the population lived close to starvation level and one in four harvests were poor so the government had to take action to prevent **food riots**. The lack of food riots, even in the 1580s and 1590s when harvests were particularly poor, suggests that measures were mostly effective.

The government passed Acts limiting the export of grain in 1534, 1555, 1559, 1563, 1571 and 1593. Measures were also taken to prevent its hoarding in 1527, 1544, 1545, 1550, 1556 and 1562. The government also issued JPs with Books of Orders in 1527, 1550, 1556 and 1586 on how to deal with shortages. Meanwhile, in the 1590s JPs were instructed on how to move corn to areas suffering from shortages.

Unemployment

Outside farming, the cloth trade was the largest employer and any decline in sales resulted in workers losing their jobs. Unemployment could cause unrest so the government took measures to regulate the trade and maintain the quality of cloth to sustain exports. The most notable piece of legislation was the 1563 Statute of Artificers, which fixed maximum wages and restricted the movement of all workers, as the unemployed travelling in search of work were seen as a threat to stability.

Social policies

The government was concerned with the rising number of poor and beggars, who were seen as a threat to law and order. Laws were passed, initially just punishing them; however, under Elizabeth Acts provided for those who were sick or old. Parishes were required to provide work for the unemployed. By the 1590s, the genuine poor were assisted, but the 'undeserving' were still punished. Although it is difficult to judge the impact of this legislation, there was very little unrest in the 1590s despite the poor economic situation.

Support or challenge?

Below is a sample exam question which asks how far you agree with a specific statement. Below this is a series of general statements which are relevant to the question. Using the information on the opposite page, page 64 and information from earlier in the book, decide whether these statements support or challenge the statement in the question and tick the appropriate box.

'Government policies destabilised England.' How far do you agree?

	Support	Challenge
Parliament voted Henry VII extra money for wars against France and Scotland in 1489 and 1497		
Statutes of 1487 and 1504 limited retaining		
Government attempt to raise Amicable Grant, 1525		
The dissolution of the smaller monasteries, 1536		
The Act of **Six Articles**, 1539		
The Enclosure Commission, 1548		
The new Prayer Book, 1549		
Introduction of penal laws against Catholics, 1571		
Reforms to the Council of the North after the rising of the Northern Earls in 1569		

 RAG – rate the timeline

Below are a sample exam question and a timeline. Using information from the page opposite, page 64 and from earlier in the book, read the question, study the timeline and, using three coloured pens, put a Red, Amber or Green star next to the events to show the following:

- **Red:** events and policies that have no relevance to the question.
- **Amber:** events and policies that have some significance to the question.
- **Green:** events and policies that are directly relevant to the question.

1 'Government legislation was the most important factor in the maintenance of political stability.' How far do you agree?

Now repeat the activity with the following questions.

2 Assess the view that Elizabeth I's reign was the most successful in the use of legislation to increase stability.

3 To what extent did government policies create political instability in the period?

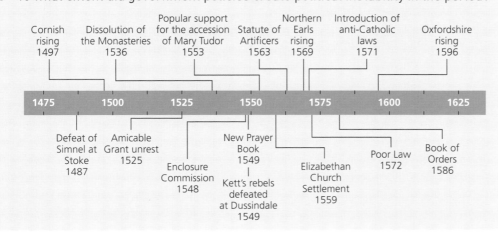

The role of parliament and councils

Parliament

Parliament passed many of the measures described on page 62, but it was not a regular part of Tudor government, meeting just thirteen times during Elizabeth's 45-year reign. It met only when the monarch summoned it and could be dissolved or **prorogued** whenever the monarch desired. However, it played a valuable role as a sounding board for policy and by the end of the period membership was a status symbol among the gentry.

The importance of parliament

Despite the limitations it did play an important role at various stages:

- Henry VII helped secure his rule through Acts of Livery and Maintenance in 1487 and 1504, which clamped down on illegal retaining, which had caused unrest.
- The House of Lords tried nobles who had been involved in rebellions, such as **Hussey** and **Darcy** after the Pilgrimage of Grace, Dacre after the Northern Earls and Essex after his rebellion.
- **Acts of Attainder** were passed; Henry VII's parliaments passed 138 Acts.
- Parliament passed legislation to protect monarchs, for example in 1571 to protect Elizabeth from Catholic plots.
- Later, parliament, rather than rebellion, was used by the **gentry** to express their grievances and to influence policy.

As the gentry became more involved in discussing issues that affected their localities, such as local law and order, the Poor Laws and economic regulations, they were less likely to lead rebellions as they had another outlet through which they could express their grievances.

Councils

At the centre was the King's Council, which became the **Privy Council** during the 1530s. There was also a series of regional councils. Their purpose was to put the monarch's wishes into practice and enforce laws. This was important in regions far from London where the king's **writ** was more difficult to enforce because of the power of local families.

The Privy Council

Under Henry VII over 200 men attended council meetings, although fewer than twenty attended regularly. By 1540 a select group formed the Privy Council, which developed as a result of the Pilgrimage of Grace and Henry's need for advice. Its importance grew under Elizabeth and by the end of the period it was meeting daily. It implemented policies such as the Elizabethan Church Settlement and the crushing of unrest in Ireland. It also carried out routine work which helped maintain stability, including organising JPs.

Regional councils

They received their orders from the council in London, but also became administrative and judicial bodies.

The Council of the North

A **Yorkist** creation, it was dominated by Yorkist families, such as the Percys. To increase his control, Henry appointed the Earl of Surrey as his representative. Surrey needed to show loyalty to get his estates restored having supported the Yorkist cause. The council was remodelled after the Pilgrimage of Grace in an attempt to increase royal control. Edward and Mary gave power back to the traditional families of the area, but after the Northern Earls rebellion Elizabeth appointed her cousin as president and there was no further unrest, despite the region's support for Catholicism.

The Council of Wales

With no very powerful landowners the region was less of a problem and there were no rebellions.

The Council of the West

Set up in 1538 following the **Exeter Conspiracy** as there was no powerful family in the region and there was also the fear of a French invasion. The council lasted only two years; unrest broke out in 1549.

The Council of Ireland

This was the least successful council. Government needed to work with **clan** chiefs to achieve stability, whereas the use of English governors created unrest.

Simple essay style

Below is a sample exam question. Use your own knowledge, information on the opposite page and information from other sections of the book to produce a plan for this question. Choose four general points, and provide three pieces of specific information to support each general point. Once you have planned your essay, write the introduction and conclusion for the essay. The introduction should list the points to be discussed in the essay **and outline the line of argument you intend to take**. The conclusion should summarise the key points and justify which point was the most important.

> To what extent did the importance of councils in the maintenance of political stability decline during the period?

Developing an argument

Read the following sample exam question, a list of key points to be made in the essay, and a paragraph from the essay. Using the information from the page opposite and from the rest of the section, rewrite the paragraph in order to develop an argument. Your paragraph should explain why the factor discussed in the paragraph is either the most significant factor or less significant than another factor.

> 'Parliament played a significant role in the maintenance of political stability.' Assess this view.

Key points:

To answer this question, you should compare and contrast the impact on stability of the following groups and institutions:

- Parliament
- Monarchy
- Royal councils
- The Church
- Nobility
- Gentry
- 'Middling sort' and lower orders

Sample paragraph:

Parliament met only when the monarch summoned it. Its most important role was in passing religious and social and economic legislation. The legislation justified the religious changes and showed that the monarch had the support of the political nation. Parliament also passed laws to try to ease food shortages in the 1590s, preventing the export of grain or ensuring through the Book of Orders that JPs had the power to distribute it where needed.

The role of the nobility

For a description of all the rebellions mentioned see pages 8–9.

The nobility played a fundamental role in the maintenance of political stability, acting as both the upholders of law and order in the localities, but also having the power and influence to undermine royal authority.

The power of the nobility

- Nobles acted as landowners, with families, such as the Percys and Howards, building up large estates where they ruled their **tenants** like kings. They were able to raise forces from their tenants which threatened the power of the monarch, but the monarch also needed these forces to put down unrest. It was therefore important to keep the nobility loyal.
- Nobles acted as local governors, often commanding the following of local gentry, which allowed them to manage local politics. As **Lord Lieutenants**, they acted as the crown's representatives in the counties, commanded the local militia and were responsible for justice. As presidents of councils they could influence justice and the raising of troops. They were particularly important in the border areas, which were not visited by monarchs.
- They held influence at court, often as friends of the monarch, but also occupying offices such as **steward** or **chamberlain**. They also had an important role on the Privy Council, although with the emergence of professional advisors such as Thomas **Cromwell** to Henry VIII and William Cecil to Elizabeth I their influence was in decline.
- They had influence in parliament, either as members of the Lords, or through influencing the election of MPs to the Commons.
- They could become disaffected and challenge the monarch, as was shown by the Earl of Essex in 1601 who objected to the domination of the low-born Cecil family.

Suppression of rebellion

The following table shows the importance of the nobility in the suppression of unrest:

Rebellion	Date	Nobles involved in suppression
Simnel	1486–87	Henry had the support of a duke, five earls, a viscount and four barons
Warbeck	1497	Earl of Devon, Lord Daubeney and Willoughby de Broke
Amicable Grant	1525	Dukes of Norfolk and Suffolk
Pilgrimage of Grace	1536	Earl of Shrewsbury, Duke of Norfolk
Western Rebellion	1549	Lord Russell
Kett's rebellion	1549	Marquis of Northampton, Earl of Warwick
Wyatt's rebellion	1554	Duke of Norfolk, Earl of Pembroke
Northern Earls	1569	Earl of Sussex, Lords Hunsdon, Warwick and Clinton
Irish rebellions	1536–1601	Lords Grey, Mountjoy and Essex

Nobility and the undermining of stability

Despite the importance of nobles in quelling unrest, throughout the period many rebellions were led or supported by nobles (see table, page 30) as they had large households and retainers, which could become a private army. When they opposed the regime it could create instability. This was particularly true in Ireland where all rebellions were led by nobles, such as the Earls of Tyrone, Kildare and Desmond.

By the end of the period, the crown did gradually weaken noble control in vulnerable areas, such as the north. The nobility became less politically ambitious and more respectful of the law.

Quick quizzes at **www.hoddereducation.co.uk/myrevisionnotes**

❗ Complete the paragraph   ⓐ

Below are a sample exam question and a paragraph written in answer to this question. The paragraph contains a point and specific examples, but lacks a concluding explanatory link back to the question. Using the information on the opposite page, on page 68 and from earlier sections of the book, complete the paragraph, adding this link in the space provided.

Assess the importance of the nobility in the maintenance of political stability.

> The nobility were important in maintaining stability in the peripheral regions of the country, particularly the north. Some families, such as the Percys, owned large amounts of land and were therefore able to rule as petty kings. They possessed a large number of tenants and were therefore able to raise considerable forces, making them indispensable in the maintenance of order. Successive monarchs sought to bring such families under control through Acts against livery and maintenance or by appointing local gentry, who owed their office to the crown, to key jobs. As Lord Lieutenants or as presidents of regional councils the nobility were vital, acting as the principal upholders of order.
>
> _____
>
> _____

❗ Delete as applicable   ⓐ

Below are a sample exam question and a paragraph written in answer to this question. Read the paragraph and decide which of the possible options (in bold) is most appropriate. Delete the least appropriate options and complete the paragraph by justifying your selection.

How far did the importance of the nobility change in the maintenance of stability in the period?

> To a **great/fair/limited** extent, the importance of the nobility changed in the maintenance of stability in the period. Henry VII was to a **great/fair/limited** extent reliant upon his nobility for the maintenance of stability. The nobility were **very/not very** important in putting down unrest as was seen by both the Simnel and Cornish risings. This pattern **changed/stayed the same** under Henry VIII when dealing with the Pilgrimage of Grace where nobles such as **Norfolk/Suffolk** were important in negotiating with the rebels. During the reigns of Edward and Elizabeth the role of the nobility in putting down disorder **changed/stayed the same** with the use of Russell in 1549 and **Sussex/Essex** in 1569. However, the nobility were also a cause of unrest; seen most noticeably in the reigns of **Henry VII/Henry VIII/Edward VI/Mary Tudor/Elizabeth** when they led rebellions. Overall, to a **great/fair/limited** extent, the importance of the nobility changed in the maintenance of stability in the period because. . .
>
> _____
>
> _____

The role of the gentry and the 'middling sort'

For a description of all the rebellions mentioned see pages 8–9.

As the sixteenth century progressed the importance of the gentry and the 'middling sort' in maintaining stability increased. Their inclusion in the running of the Tudor state meant that they no longer provided leadership for rebellions, as had happened with Kett and Wyatt, but instead worked for the state. It can be argued that this change explains why rebellions after 1549 attracted such small numbers and why peasant rebellions, such as Oxfordshire (1596), were poorly led.

The gentry

The most important role of the gentry was as Justices of the Peace (JPs), providing a pivotal link between the crown and counties. Although JPs had existed in the fourteenth century, their work and numbers increased dramatically in the period 1485–1603. The absence of major rebellions after 1570 may not be solely due to their existence, but they did ensure that the government was better informed and able to respond to local crises, such as the food shortages in the 1590s.

As JPs they had two main roles:
- Judicial: They dispensed justice at a local level, committing to jail those who disturbed the peace and therefore preventing local disturbances from developing into rebellion. They could detain and punish rioters and resolve disputes between masters and servants.
- Administrative: They ensured that statutes were enforced, most importantly the price of grain during food shortages and overseeing the welfare of the poor, both of which were vital in the harsh economic climate of the 1590s.

These roles increased the status of the gentry and, as some also became MPs, moved them up the social ladder. This ensured that they had more in common with the ruling elites than the peasantry, thus encouraging them to remain loyal to the state.

The 'middling sort'

The 'middling sort' were men below the status of gentry, the yeomen farmers. Their income was less than the gentry, but they were growing richer. They were often the largest landowners within villages and, as such, seen as the village elites.

In the latter part of the period it was the 'middling sort' who took on roles such as **churchwardens**, **bailiffs**, **constables** and **overseers of the poor**, giving them a significant measure of local control. This increased their status within their communities, ensuring, like the gentry, they had more in common with the higher orders in society. Consequently, the 'middling sort' became increasingly suspicious of the poor and the threat they posed.

Their incorporation into the national political culture meant that the Tudor state could count on the support of an increasing number of men who put loyalty to the state above loyalty to their local communities. This was demonstrated in the lack of support for the Oxfordshire rising in 1596. Those who held local offices had a vested interest in supporting the state and maintaining rather than challenging order.

Support or challenge?

Below is a sample exam question which asks how far you agree with a specific statement. Below this is a series of general statements which are relevant to the question. Using the information on the opposite page and from the rest of the book, decide whether these statements support or challenge the statement in the question and tick the appropriate box.

'The maintenance of stability owed much to the "middling sort".' How far do you agree?

	Support	Challenge
The dynastic rebellions under Henry VII were defeated by royal and noble forces		
Local government was firmly in the hands of the nobility at the start of the period		
The 'middling sort' were active in the Amicable Grant unrest		
The nobility were important in the maintenance of stability as they led royal forces		
Many of the Western Rebels were from just below the ruling groups		
Robert Kett was a **yeoman**		
Thomas Wyatt was a member of the gentry class		
The development of institutions such as parliament increased the role of the gentry in government		
JPs carried out essential judicial and administrative work that helped to maintain stability		
The later period saw a reformation in manners (see page 70)		
The Oxfordshire rising attracted little support		
During Elizabeth's reign the 'middling sort' acted as overseers of the poor and churchwardens		

Simple essay style

Below is a sample exam question. Use your own knowledge, information on the opposite page and information from other sections of the book to produce a plan for this question. Choose four general points, and provide three pieces of specific information to support each general point. Once you have planned your essay, write the introduction and conclusion for the essay. The introduction should list the points to be discussed in the essay **and outline the line of argument you intend to take.** The conclusion should summarise the key points and justify which point was the most important.

Assess the role of the gentry in maintaining political stability in England and Ireland.

Popular attitudes to authority

For a description of all the rebellions mentioned see pages 8–9.

Tudor monarchs had no **standing army** or police force to maintain order. Although they developed a series of institutions that helped enforce peace, they also relied on respect. Respect for authority was based on a range of concepts, from the sin of rebelling against a monarch appointed by God, to respect for the head of the household.

The Divine Right of Kings

Although Tudor monarchs did not fully develop the concept of the **Divine Right of Kings**, they did use the idea that they were appointed by God to help create a sense of mystique and respect. God had appointed sovereigns and expected them to be obeyed. Even Henry VII, who had won the throne on the battlefield, claimed he was 'Henry, by the grace of God, King'. However, this concept had less impact when the country was ruled by a **Protector** or **Lord President**, such as in the period 1547–53.

The Great Chain of Being

The **Great Chain of Being** suggested that everyone was born into a set place in society and that the order was unfaltering. It also taught the themes of loyalty, duty and obligation. However, this applied to those at the top of society as well as the bottom and did not always help in the preservation of peace as the lower orders might look to their superiors for leadership when rebelling, as in the Pilgrimage of Grace, 1536.

Society of Orders

The Society of Orders also suggested that everyone had their place and role in society. However, this could encourage disquiet if it appeared that the government was showing contempt for the Society of Orders, or if gentlemen failed to perform their expected duties. This happened in the rebellions of 1549, when the rebels complained that the gentry were exploiting the economic conditions and not offering help to the lower orders.

The household

The structure of the family helped to uphold the concept of hierarchy and law and order. This was very useful as it was enforced daily. The head of the house was to be obeyed and those who resisted were made to conform. The Church supported this, teaching that obedience to the head of the household was required by God. The family was seen as mirroring the state, with the head of the house the equivalent of the monarch, thus reinforcing the idea of obedience.

A reformation of manners?

The period may also have witnessed a change in attitudes and behaviour, encouraged by the religious developments of the later period. This 'reformation in manners' resulted in people trying to control their behaviour, using litigation rather than unrest to settle disputes and showing a greater willingness to compromise. This development was encouraged by families often praying and reading the Bible together, which helped to reinforce the importance of the household and hierarchy. This had a particular impact on the wealthier elements of society.

As the gulf between the rich and poor widened over the century the more prosperous discovered that they had less in common with the labourers and peasantry. The wealthy, who owned property, had an interest in upholding order, rather than leading riots. Therefore, by the end of the period, the political nation had grown to include a significant proportion of the population who adopted collective responsibility for the maintenance of law and order.

Turning assertion into argument a

Below are a sample question and a series of assertions. Read the exam question and then add a justification to each of the assertions to turn each one into an argument.

How important were changing attitudes to disorder in maintaining stability?

Respect for authority was important to Tudor governments because...

_____

_____

Changing attitudes to disorder were also essential in maintaining stability because...

_____

_____

Moreover, the gulf between the rich and poor helped maintain stability because...

_____

_____

Recommended reading

Below is a list of suggested further reading on this topic.

- Nicholas Fellows, *Access to History: Disorder and Rebellion in Tudor England*, Hodder Education (2001), pages 4–7
- Steve Hindle, *The State and Social Change in Early Modern England 1550–1640*, Palgrave Macmillan (2002), Chapters 7 and 8
- Paul Thomas, Cambridge Perspectives in History: *Authority and Disorder in Tudor Times, 1485–1603*, CUP (1999)

Exam focus

Below is a sample high-level essay in response to an exam-style question. Read the essay and the comments around it.

How far did England become more politically stable during the period from 1485 to 1603?

In 1485 Henry Tudor seized the throne on the battlefield, yet in 1603 on the death of Elizabeth, the throne was passed on peacefully, despite Elizabeth dying childless, suggesting that at least the succession was more stable. Similarly, the decline in the frequency and severity of unrest in the period after 1549 also supports the view that England was more stable. Riot and rebellion were no longer the methods used by most to resolve differences, instead parliament or litigation was more popular. However, despite these developments, there was still some instability as factional disputes continued throughout the period.

There is a clear line of argument and a series of themes which can be built on are introduced. The last sentence suggests that the argument will be balanced.

The decline in the frequency and severity of rebellion suggests England was more politically stable by 1603. Rebellion had been a common feature of Henry VII's reign, even being forced into battle against Simnel to defend his throne, but under Elizabeth there were only three rebellions, with the Northern Earls the most serious, attracting 5000 supporters. When this is compared to the Pilgrimage of Grace in 1536, which attracted 40,000 rebels, it is clear that the appeal of rebellion had declined. Moreover, the two rebellions towards the end of Elizabeth's reign attracted even less support; the Oxfordshire rising attracting only five and Essex defeated in under twelve hours, whereas both the Western and Kett's rebellions in 1549 lasted over a month. However, it should be remembered that Essex had still been able to raise a rebellion in Elizabeth's capital city, suggesting that stability was not completely assured.

There is clear evidence of a synoptic approach with comparison between the start and end of the period. There is some strong synthesis and again balance to the argument.

Early rebellions presented a far greater threat to stability. Many were politically motivated and aimed to overthrow the monarch, with Lovell, Stafford, Simnel and Warbeck all aiming to replace Henry VII with a Yorkist claimant. These political challenges continued until 1553 with Northumberland's attempt to replace Mary Tudor with Lady Jane Grey. However, political stability increased as low politics replaced high politics as a cause of unrest. Politically motivated rebellions gave way to economically driven unrest, which was less threatening as it lacked support from the nobility or gentry. Despite this, factional disputes continued throughout, with attempts in 1536 by the Aragonese faction to regain influence, in 1553 as Northumberland tried to maintain power, in 1554 when Wyatt attempted to limit Spanish influence and in the Essex rebellion of 1601, resulting from the domination of the Cecils. However, despite these struggles, the regime was not destabilised, as even in 1549 the transition of power to Northumberland as Lord President of the Council was smooth, suggesting that even at potential crisis points stability was far greater than in 1486 when Henry had to fight for his throne.

The focus is on change and continuity, with the response showing England was less stable at the start than the end of the period. The discussion is balanced.

Stability was also increased by the decline in religious conflict which had been a feature of the mid-Tudor period. Initially religion had been a bond holding society together, but the changes that followed the break with Rome created instability, with the Pilgrimage of Grace, the Western Rebellion and the Northern Earls seeking to preserve their traditional religious practices and institutions. The Elizabethan broad-based church did much to reduce religious tension, reflected in the lack of support for the papal bull of 1570, which excommunicated Elizabeth, or the Armada in 1588.

The focus on continuity and change continues. However, a judgement would have helped strengthen the paragraph.

The change in the role of the nobility helped bring about increased political stability. Instead of fighting, as had happened during the reigns of Henry VII and Henry VIII, Elizabeth's nobles were more willing to serve the state, and saw the monarch as the source of rewards. Under the early Tudors, the nobility were able to raise large forces of retainers and directly challenge the monarch, but under Elizabeth noble unrest was the last resort of the desperate, as with Northumberland, Westmorland and Essex, all of whom felt so excluded from power that they had nothing to lose. However, nobles were more likely to be found on the side of the monarch. They supplied troops to crush unrest, as with Hunsdon and Sussex in 1569, acted as Lord Lieutenants to prevent the outbreak of rebellion, or negotiated with rebels as Arundel did in 1549. Many nobles had increased their wealth and had too much to lose in rebelling. Instead, they used the law courts or parliament to resolve disputes. Their unwillingness to be involved in unrest also deprived potential rebels of leadership and further increased stability.

The response continues to compare the start and end of the period. The last sentence links the argument back to the question.

Similarly, both the gentry and the 'middling sort' had, by the end of the period, allied themselves with the crown and were unwilling to lead rebellions, unlike 1549 or 1554 with Kett and Wyatt. As a consequence, the crown had the support of the political nation. The growing use of parliament as a sounding board for policy involved many in decision making and membership became a status symbol that they were unwilling to risk losing through revolting. Those just below gentry status also gained from the rewards of office-holding. The 'middling sort' became churchwardens, Poor Law Commissioners and parish constables, raising their status within their communities and distancing themselves from the lower orders. Their incorporation in the state and realisation that their interests were better served by supporting it significantly reduced the potential for unrest and increased stability.

This builds on the previous paragraph and explains how winning over other elements increased stability.

Even among the lower orders there became less inclination to rebel. It appeared as if they had realised that rebellion usually ended in failure and often death. The events of Dussindale and Clyst Heath were a reminder that rebellion was not an effective way to resolve disputes. Their lives were already nasty, brutish and short and there was no need to add to this by rioting, which may explain why only five men turned up for the 1596 Oxfordshire rising.

The argument continues, but there could have been a stronger link back to the question.

The growth and development of governing institutions and bodies throughout the period, such as the Privy Council, councils in the regions, parliament and the development of offices, such as Lord Lieutenant, all helped to increase government control and ensure that laws were enforced and upheld. The Tudor monarchy became more stable the longer it ruled, shown in its ability to survive the weak rule of Edward VI and Mary I. There were disputes, even in the last years of Elizabeth's reign, and the threat of invasion from the war with Spain, but the monarch had the support of more of the nation than had been the case in 1485, making England much more stable than it had been.

The conclusion reflects the line of argument pursued throughout the essay and although the institutional developments mentioned in this paragraph could have been developed as a separate issue, the answer has covered a wide range of issues and themes and it would be unrealistic to expect everything to be covered in the time allowed.

A very strong answer but there are some slightly weaker areas, as in the section on religion or the penultimate paragraph, which prevent it from reaching the very top. However, it is well organised and easy to follow, with a balanced discussion, leading to a well-supported conclusion.

What makes a good synoptic answer?

You have now considered four sample A grade essays. Use these essays to make a bullet-point list of the characteristics of an A grade synoptic essay. Use this list when planning and writing your own practice exam essays.

5 Depth study: The Pilgrimage of Grace

The causes of the Pilgrimage of Grace

No Tudor rebellion has engendered more debate about its causes than the Pilgrimage of Grace. Traditionally seen as a religious rebellion, the work of some historians, most notably Geoffrey Elton, has challenged this view.

Religious causes

The religious demands made up 9 out of the 24 grievances and were at the head of their list of demands, suggesting that religion was their primary concern.

- The demands attacked many recent changes and attacked traditional religious practices, including the abolition of holy days and saints' days.
- They attacked the new taxes of baptisms, burials and marriages, which it was claimed the poorer elements in society could not afford.
- They attacked reformist bishops, such as **Thomas Cranmer**, and also European reformers, such as Martin Bucer.

The rising came soon after the smaller monasteries in the region had been closed and in Lancashire the rising was centred around the areas where monasteries had been dissolved. It was also in these areas where the rising continued for the longest.

The symbols of the rising were religious:

- The rebels' banner depicted the **Five Wounds of Christ**.
- The **Pilgrims' ballad** and oath contained a strong religious message. The oath stated that they were undertaking the Pilgrimage in the name of Christ.

Political causes

- Elton argued that the Pilgrimage was the result of court **faction**. He argued that the **Aragonese** faction, supporters of Henry's first wife **Catherine of Aragon**, had been defeated in both court and parliament following the fall of Catherine and the break with Rome. In order to try to regain their influence they raised a popular rebellion.
- Henry VIII's centralising policy, by which feudal ties in the north had been undermined, further angered some. Those who were involved in the rebellion were the men who had lost out because of this policy and included Lords **Hussey** and **Darcy**.

- The north appeared to be excluded from decision making and therefore the rebels asked for a parliament in the north.
- The traditional advisors of the king had been replaced by men such as Cranmer, **Thomas Cromwell** and Richard Rich, who are all attacked in the Pilgrims' ballad.
- The rebels asked for the restoration of Mary to the succession and a parliament in the north.

Economic causes

Economic grievances were present among the rebels' demands.

- They complained about the 1534 **Subsidy Act**, which attempted to raise money in peace time and came at a time of poverty, with poor harvests in 1535 and 1536.
- They complained about enclosure, which was a serious problem in the more populated areas of the Lake District and the West Riding of Yorkshire.
- There was a complaint about **entry fines**.
- Added to the demands, there were also rumours of new taxes being brought in on sheep and cattle.

Was it a multi-causal rebellion?

Contemporaries would not have categorised the rebellion and it might be better to see it either as multi-causal or a response to changes that affected northern society. This is best seen through the closure of the smaller monasteries. This would have had a religious impact as they often acted as local churches and therefore provided spiritual support. They also had an economic impact, providing employment and a market for goods. Lastly, they were important socially in an area that was affected by poverty as they provided charity and education and acted as a hospital and an inn for travellers. Therefore, their closure had a major impact on northern society.

How far do you agree?

Read Passage A, then use your own knowledge to agree with, or to challenge the argument.

Argument in passage	Knowledge that corroborates	Knowledge that disagrees
1		
2		
3		

PASSAGE A

The causes of the Pilgrimage of Grace. Adapted from C. Haigh, English Reformations: Religion, Politics and Society under the Tudors *(1993)*

The secular demands were late additions to the basic religious grievances, rather than vice versa, and it was the local impact of Henry's **Reformation** which had produced the rebellion. When the commons were active in rebellion, it was not in refusing rents or pulling down enclosures; it was in protesting at the abolition of traditional religious practices, or in forcing nervous priests to pray for the pope. However, it was not the suppression of papal authority that brought violent conflict, it was the suppression of monasteries. Laymen did not fight for the papal primacy, nor for the liberties of the Church; they did not take risks to protect the clergy from royal taxes or royal visitation.

Above all the commons defended and restored monasteries. As early as mid-September four parishes in the Yorkshire Dales had taken an oath to protect the monasteries, some chased off suppression commissioners. In all, the rebels restored at least sixteen of the twenty-six northern monasteries that had actually been dissolved.

Summarise the arguments

Below are a sample exam question and one of the passages referred to in the question. Read Passage B and identify the interpretation offered. Look for the arguments of the passage.

> Evaluate the interpretations in both of the two passages and explain which you think is more convincing as an explanation of the causes of the Pilgrimage of Grace.

Interpretation offered by the passage:

_____

_____

_____

_____

PASSAGE B

Adapted from G.R. Elton, Reform and Reformation; England 1509–1558 *(1977)*

The Pilgrimage originated in a decision by one of the court factions to take the battle out of the court into the nation, to raise the standard of loyal rebellion as the only way left to them if they were to succeed in reversing the defeats suffered at court and in parliament, and in forcing the king to change his policy. In the plotting around the imperial ambassador this leadership had not been alone; the ambassador compiled a long list of allegedly disaffected noblemen willing to join in rebellion against Henry.

The nature of the Pilgrimage of Grace

The debate centres around who actually led the Lincolnshire rising and the Pilgrimage of Grace. There has been disagreement over the extent to which it was led by an out-of-favour court faction, involving men such as Lord Hussey (see page 16), or whether it was leaders of local society or a protest of the commons.

Court faction

The nobility and gentry who were involved in the rising certainly had motives to take up arms and lead a rising:

● They had lost their position at court and disliked the influence of Thomas Cromwell and Anne Boleyn.
● Hussey and Darcy had court connections and played key roles in the actual rising. Hussey had been Mary's **chamberlain** and had lost his office and his wife had been imprisoned for encouraging Mary to resist the Royal Supremacy.
● The centralising policy of Henry had undermined their positions in northern society. Outsiders, such as the Duke of Suffolk, had been given large amounts of land in Lincolnshire.

Gentry

The organisation of the rebellion suggests that it was not spontaneous. Only the gentry had the ability and connections to organise such a large-scale protest. Their position was affected by the policy of centralisation, losing out to men such as Cromwell and Rich, men they viewed as upstarts.

Some of the rebel demands also suggest that it was led by the gentry:

● The **Statute of Uses** would affect only them.
● The names of some of the **heretics** attacked in the grievances, such as Ecolampadius and Rastall, would not have been familiar to the commons.

However, the gentry argued they were coerced into leading the rebellion. Some suggested that their families and property were threatened. But this was a useful excuse once the rising had failed and they faced punishments.

The commons

A detailed study of the rebel armies by Michael Bush (1996) showed that the Pilgrimage was primarily 'a movement of the commons'. He argues the commons pressurised the gentry to lead the rising. This gave it greater legitimacy and because they were the natural leaders of society they would be best able to put across their views.

The importance of the commons in the protest is also reflected in the original name of the movement, 'pilgrimage for grace for the commonwealth'. This was also reflected in the aims as they argued that they wanted to protect the commonwealth. This explains why they were concerned about taxation, **tenants**' rights and the wealth of local churches.

It would appear that in Lincolnshire the original leaders were the richer **yeomen** and tradesmen; the men who would have been **churchwardens** and **parish constables**.

Clergy

Clergy and monks played a significant role in the rising. This might be expected as their lives had been hit the most by the changes. At Louth, where it started, the priest encouraged the rising, although it was originally led by a cobbler, Nicholas Melton. The clergy supplied money for the rising, whilst some monks also joined and were armed and horsed.

The rising involved a wide range of social groups and each with their own grievances. Historians have failed to reach agreement as to whether it was a rising of the commons aided by the gentry or of the gentry assisted by the commons. However, the scale and cross-class support suggests that the whole of northern society was out of joint.

Summarise the arguments

Below are a sample exam question and one of the passages referred to in the question. Read Passage A and identify the interpretation offered. Look for the arguments of the passage.

> Evaluate the interpretations in both of the two passages and explain which you think is more convincing as an explanation of the nature of those involved in the Pilgrimage of Grace.

Interpretation offered by the passage:

_____

_____

_____

PASSAGE A

Adapted from G.R. Elton, Reform and Reformation: England 1509–1558 *(1977)*

In short, the Pilgrimage, though it had its spontaneous moments, was in itself no spontaneous event but in great measure a planned rising. The point is proved by a look at the real leaders who did not come from either the commons or the great northern families. The three chiefs were Darcy, Constable and Hussey, with Aske providing a cover for them. These were the men who really organised the rising – the remnant of the Aragonese party. The idea of a spontaneous combustion which then brought in the existing inflammatory material to set the whole north ablaze is not in accord with the facts; it is necessary to regard the evidence of manifest advance planning.

How far do you agree?

Read Passage B, then use your own knowledge to agree with, or to challenge the argument.

Argument in passage	Knowledge that corroborates	Knowledge that disagrees
1		
2		
3		

PASSAGE B

The nature of the rebel armies in 1536. Adapted from Michael Bush, The Pilgrimage of Grace: A Study of the Rebel Armies of October 1536 *(1996)*

The armies of 1536 were undoubtedly part of a long tradition. As the product of the so-called risings of the commons, which aimed to put the government right, they belonged to a genre of protest that had its beginnings in 1381 (the **Peasants' Revolt**) and that came to spectacular fruition between 1489 and 1549. In these rebellions the armies acted in the name and interest of the commons ... Within this tradition of revolt, the northern rising was distinctive. It recruited from the whole range of society, their supporters including gentlemen and clerics as well as townsmen and peasants. Some of the participants claimed they were forced to join, but clearly evident was not only a fury of all three orders but also their ability to find common accord. None of these armies or hosts was the work of one particular social group.

The impact of the Pilgrimage of Grace

The period after the Pilgrimage of Grace suggests that Henry slowed down religious change as he feared further unrest. However, some have argued that he increased the pace as he could not trust the monks or clergy who were blamed for the unrest.

Change slowed down

The Bishops' Book of 1537 was conservative and restored many traditional practices, restoring the four lost sacraments from the Ten Articles of 1536. The Act of **Six Articles** of 1539 also confirmed a number of Catholic practices, including transubstantiation. The cautious and largely conservative religious policy continued into the 1540s, with radical preaching attacked. The architect of many of the religious changes, Thomas Cromwell, was removed from power in 1540 and this may have been due to his more radical religious beliefs.

Religious change speeded up

This argument is supported most clearly by the dissolution of the larger monasteries. Henry went against his promise to allow the smaller monasteries to stand until a parliament in the north met, but he closed all monasteries, despite having praised the larger ones in 1536. The Pilgrimage led him to see the monks as disloyal and owing obedience to the pope. Despite some evidence of the pace of change slowing down there were still some reformist moves with the publication of the Great Bible in 1539 and **Injunctions** in 1538, which discouraged pilgrimages and ordered **relics** to be removed from churches, a further attack on the Catholic belief in purgatory.

As the largest of all Tudor rebellions and outnumbering government forces five to one, as well as a challenge to government policy, it was seen as a serious threat.

Threat to the Tudor regime

The Pilgrims had raised some 40,000 rebels, but the government could raise a force of only 8000, which forced Henry and his commander, the Duke of Norfolk, to negotiate and play for time. The threat was increased as the rebels took York, the second city, and Pontefract Castle, seen as the 'gateway to the south'. As royal authority in the north was also less strong and the loyalty of some northern nobles dubious it meant the rebellion could not be put down locally. The rebellion had also been able to draw support from all classes of society, which could make it a similar threat to that posed by the Amicable Grant.

The rebellion was also a direct challenge to government policies, attacking both religion and the succession, and therefore the government could not afford to make major concessions; it was this that was the greatest challenge. The government response certainly adds weight to this view. The government was also worried about political stability in the region and reformed the **Council of the North**, whilst Henry took on the role of warden of the Marches of lands bordering Scotland. Unable to trust the nobility, he brought in gentry as his deputies.

The government did make concessions over the **subsidy** and regulated **entry fines**, giving way on economic issues, but not over religious or political ones.

Support your judgement

Read the following sample exam question and two basic judgements. Support the judgement that you agree with more strongly by adding a reason and evidence that justifies the judgement.

> Evaluate the interpretations and explain which you think is the more convincing explanation of the impact of the Pilgrimage of Grace.

Answer 1:

The Pilgrimage of Grace had a profound impact on the government's religious legislation and convincing Henry that monasteries and monks were the focal point of opposition to his religious changes.

Answer 2:

The Pilgrimage of Grace had little impact on the direction or pace of the English Reformation.

Tip: Whichever option you choose you will have to weigh up both sides of the argument. You could use words such as 'whereas' or 'although' in order to help the process of evaluation.

 Recommended reading

- Michael Bush, *The Pilgrimage of Grace: A Study of the Rebel Armies of October 1536*, MUP (1996)
- C.S.L. Davies, 'The Pilgrimage of Grace Reconsidered', *Past and Present 41* (1968)
- G.R. Elton, *Reform and Reformation; England 1509–1558*, Arnold (1977), Chapter 11
- Nicholas Fellows, *Disorder and Rebellion in Tudor England*, Hodder (2001)
- A. Fletcher and D. MacCulloch, *Tudor Rebellions*, Pearson Longman (2015)
- C. Haigh, *Reformation and Resistance in Tudor Lancashire*, CUP (1976)
- R.W. Hoyle, *The Pilgrimage of Grace and the Politics of the 1530s*, OUP (2001)
- G. Moorhouse, *The Pilgrimage of Grace*, Weidenfeld and Nicolson (2002)
- Geoff Woodward and Nicholas Fellows, *Rebellion and Disorder under the Tudors*, Hodder (2016)

Exam focus

Below is a sample high-level essay on the Pilgrimage of Grace in response to an exam-style question. Read the essay and the comments around it.

Evaluate the interpretations in the two passages and explain which you think is the more convincing explanation of the causes of the Pilgrimage of Grace.

PASSAGE A

Adapted from G.R. Elton, Reform and Reformation *(1977)*

The common view sees the rebellion as the protest of a whole community – 'northern society' – against the breach with Rome and especially the Dissolution of the Monasteries, against the new learning and the king's autocracy, complicated by the social and economic grievances of its various component parts. The Pontefract Articles, which most fully sum up the aims of the movement, range comprehensively enough. The largest set of demands touched religion, but there must be grave doubts whether the articles constitute anything like a representative programme, and worse doubts about the extent to which the rebellion as a whole arose from the issues they enshrined.

The Pilgrimage originated in a decision by one of the court factions to take the battle out of the court into the nation, to raise the standard of loyal rebellion as the only way left to them if they were to succeed in reversing the defeats suffered at court and in parliament, and in forcing the king to change his policy. In the plotting around the imperial ambassador this leadership had not been alone; the ambassador compiled a long list of allegedly disaffected noblemen willing to join in rebellion against Henry.

PASSAGE B

Adapted from C. Haigh, English Reformations: Religion, Politics and Society under the Tudors *(1993)*

The twenty-four Pontefract Articles were compiled from complaints sent from all over the north, and were agreed by the assembly of representatives. They embraced many divergent interests: there were three economic articles; six on legal and administrative matters; six political articles and nine dealt with religious grievances.

The secular demands were late additions to the basic religious grievances, rather than vice versa, and it was the local impact of Henry's Reformation which had produced the rebellion. When the commons were active in rebellion, it was not in refusing rents or pulling down enclosures; it was in protesting at the abolition of traditional religious practices, or in forcing nervous priests to pray for the pope. However, it was not the suppression of papal authority that brought violent conflict, it was the suppression of monasteries. Laymen did not fight for the papal primacy, nor for the liberties of the Church; they did not take risks to protect the clergy from royal taxes or royal visitation.

Above all the commons defended and restored monasteries. As early as mid-September four parishes in the Yorkshire Dales had taken an oath to protect the monasteries, some chased off suppression commissioners. In all, the rebels restored at least sixteen of the twenty-six northern monasteries that had actually been dissolved.

The two passages acknowledge that the rising was caused by a variety of reasons. However, they differ in their view as to the most important factor in bringing about the Pilgrimage. Passage A argues that it 'originated in a decision by one of the court factions to take the battle out of the court into the nation', whilst Passage B puts forward the view that it was the 'local impact of Henry's Reformation which produced the rebellion', most notably the dissolution of the smaller monasteries and the loss of traditional religious practices.

The opening paragraph clearly outlines the views of the two interpretations, aware of both their similarities and differences.

Passage A is correct to argue that one of the court factions, the Aragonese, had suffered defeats at court with the passing of the 1534 Succession Act which excluded Mary from the throne in favour of Elizabeth. It is also true that the key figures in the rising, Aske, Darcy and Hussey, were closely associated with Catherine of Aragon and her daughter, with Hussey having been Mary's chamberlain. It is possible that Passage

A is correct in that these men were willing to use rebellion to restore their positions. More importantly, Passage A ignores the fact that Hussey stayed largely on the sidelines. Similarly, there are some weaknesses in the claim that the rising was led and organised by this faction. In light of this claim, Aske's deposition that he had been forced into the rising makes no sense, unless one accepts that he was trying to save himself. Passage A also argues that rebellion was the only way left to reverse the defeats this group had suffered, yet the initiative for the rising lay not with this group, but with popular unrest as seen in Lincolnshire, where the rising surprised many of the gentry who later became involved. Therefore, although some of the grievances make more sense if court politics were the main cause, Passage A undermines its own view by stating that 'there must be grave doubts about the extent to which the articles constitute anything like a representative programme, and worse doubts about the extent to which rebellion as a whole arose from the issues they enshrined'.

> The strengths and weaknesses of Passage A are evaluated using detailed own knowledge. A judgement about A is also reached.

However, Passage B challenges the view in A and argues that the dissolution of the smaller monasteries was the main cause. It notes that 'the rebels restored at least sixteen of the twenty-six northern monasteries that had been dissolved', seen not just in the actions of the Pilgrims in Cumbria, where all four monasteries were restored. The centrality of the dissolution put forward in Passage B is justifiable. It was the monks of Sawley who composed the Pilgrims' ballad and in Lancashire the first areas to rise and the last to be suppressed were areas where there were monasteries, suggesting that the geography of the rising supports Passage B. This view is given further credence by the Pontefract Articles which specifically mentioned their restoration, but symbols such as the badge of the Five Wounds of Christ, and comments made by Aske under examination also support the view that religion was the main cause. This is not surprising as monasteries played more than a religious role in the lives of people, they provided employment, charity, education and were often local landowners; thus although Passage B is correct to stress their importance, this claim could have been developed to include their social and economic importance. Passage B is also correct in arguing people were concerned about the loss of traditional religious practices, seen at Kirkby Stephen, where they complained about the loss of saints' days. The rebellion was largely a protest against the attacks on traditional religious practices, which Passage B correctly suggests.

> Interpretation B is evaluated using detailed knowledge, although the response does not consider any potential weaknesses of it.

Both passages correctly acknowledge that the rebellion was multi-causal and refer to social and economic concerns, which are reflected in the rebels' demands. However, they differ in their view of the main cause and whilst Passage A is useful in presenting a political interpretation, there are too many flaws in this argument to be convincing. Passage B, however, argues for religion as the main cause and, given the dominance of religious grievances in the demands, the symbolism and the actions of the rebels in restoring monastic houses this is more convincing as an interpretation of the rising.

> A supported judgement as to which is the more valid interpretation is reached. The response acknowledges the strengths of both interpretations but justifies its view that B is stronger.

The response has a clear understanding of the views of both passages and is focused on the views they offer about the causes of the Pilgrimage of Grace. The views are clearly explained and evaluated by the application of specific and relevant knowledge. A judgement as to which is more convincing is reached and is clearly supported.

Exam focus activity

Although the response contains relevant own knowledge, use the information in this section to make a list of other relevant own knowledge that could be used to evaluate the passages.

6 Depth study: The Western Rebellion

The causes of the Western Rebellion

The Western Rebellion, which gripped Devon and Cornwall in the summer of 1549, is frequently known as the **Prayer Book** Rebellion, suggesting that religion – and the new 1549 Prayer Book – was the main cause. Although this appears to be reflected in the rebels' demands, other evidence would suggest that such an interpretation is too simplistic.

Religious causes

There is certainly a great deal of evidence to suggest that the rising was caused by the religious changes introduced at the start of Edward VI's reign. The demands were religious:

- They wanted a restoration of traditional practices, such as holy bread and water, and this is reflected in the call for the restoration of the Act of **Six Articles**.
- They wanted traditional doctrine restored as the rebels asserted their belief in transubstantiation and purgatory.
- The demands attacked Protestantism. The rebels attacked communion in both kinds and the new Prayer Book, refusing to receive the new service, which they described as a 'Christmas game'. Although the rebels would not have understood the Latin mass, they wanted it restored, claiming that they did not understand the English version as they spoke Cornish.
- The rebels wanted Richard Crispin and John Moreman, two local Catholic preachers, to be released from jail so that they could preach.

However, what is noticeable is that there were no calls for the restoration of papal authority. The rebellion was still religiously conservative, but that is not surprising as it appears as if the grievances were drawn up by the clergy and were therefore bound to have a religious dimension.

Social and economic causes

Despite the dominance of religious grievances in the demands, earlier sets of grievances, that have not survived, were drawn up and these had a much more social and economic focus. They contained references to the new **Sheep and Cloth tax**, which would have hit the two counties severely, and made reference to the problem of **enclosure**. The actions of the rebels add to the view that social and economic grievances were a major issue. In particular, the actions of the rebels suggest that they were motivated by a hatred of the gentry:

- They attacked and robbed the **gentry** on St Michael's Mount.
- At Bodmin they shouted, 'Kill the gentlemen'.
- The rebels murdered William Hellyons, the only member of the gentry to resist.
- They plundered Trematon Castle.

This view of social causes was reinforced by government actions, with government forces setting fire to rebel defences at Crediton and prompting the historian, Barrett L. Beer, to comment that 'the charred barns and houses stood as a grim reminder of the widening cleavage between the landowning gentry and the masses of working men and women'.

The local authority in Exeter was also concerned about social issues as it took action to prevent the poorer elements in the city handing it over to the rebels, selling them cheap firewood and food.

Political causes

The rebels demanded the restoration of Cardinal Pole, not as a religious leader but as a political leader, demanding he was restored to the King's Council. His involvement, and the links of Richard Crispin to the **Yorkist** cause, raised fears that this was an attempt to reassert the cause of the white rose.

Therefore, this suggests that it was more than a religious rebellion and was possibly hijacked by the clergy to advance their grievances.

How far do you agree?

Read Passage A, then use your own knowledge to agree with, or to challenge the argument.

Argument in passage	Knowledge to corroborate the argument	Knowledge to challenge the argument

PASSAGE A

Adapted from C. Haigh, English Reformations: Religion, Politics and Society under the Tudors *(1993)*

The response from the parishes to the new Prayer Book was hostile, especially as it was introduced at a time of widespread grievances about taxation and agricultural change. The motives of the Western Rebels were certainly mixed. There was economic discontent, and a hostility against gentry who had co-operated with government policy. But religion was at least the common grievance which held the rebels together, and the Prayer Book was the issue which turned local disorder into regional rebellion ... The Catholic cry was not limited to the clergy and rebel leaders would not have agreed to a programme which focused almost entirely on a fringe issue. The Western rising was a determined protest against Somerset's policies, especially, but not exclusively, on religion.

Using knowledge to support or contradict

Read Passage B below. Summarise the evidence about the causes of the Western Rebellion and then develop a counter-argument:

Interpretation offered by the passage:

_____

_____

Counter-argument:

_____

_____

PASSAGE B

Adapted from Barrett L. Beer, Rebellion and Riot *(1982)*

The rebellions of 1549 occurred in an atmosphere of economic distress, for people of all ranks and degrees suffered from rising prices and a poor harvest. The growing shortage of arable and pastoral lands, caused by an increasing rural population, affected the poor most adversely and set peasants against landlords. Although a generalised description of social conditions does not by itself establish a cause for the Western Rebellion, the circumstances of the Western Rebellion and the behaviour of the rebels point towards social conflict as the cause.

The nature of the Western Rebellion

The Western Rebellion was one of the more violent of the Tudor rebellions; even the grievances, expressed as 'We will have' suggest an aggressive nature. The rebels put up strong resistance, and it took five battles or significant skirmishes to put down the unrest. However, how far this aggressive attitude was prompted by the hostility of government forces is a matter for debate.

The violence of the rebels

In the last section (page 82) we have seen that the rebels were aggressive in their behaviour towards the gentry, shouting abuse at them, attacking and even murdering the one member of the gentry who resisted. The rebels were unwilling to negotiate with the gentry, despite some gentry having sympathy with the religious demand that there should not be changes from Henry VIII's reign until Edward VI came of age.

Although the rebels did not take the regional capital, Exeter, there were a number of clashes between the city and the rebels. The rebels attempted to set fire to the city gates and mine the walls so that they could gain entry. If that had succeeded the city may have been treated in the same way as Kett's rebels behaved in Norwich, with part of it set on fire.

The rebels were willing to confront government forces and there were significant encounters at Fenny Bridges, Clyst St Mary, Clyst Heath and Sampford Courtenay before the rising was finally crushed.

The attitude and action of the government and its forces

The attitude and actions of the government and some of its officials provoked and encouraged a violent reaction from the rebels.

The impact of Courtenay's fall

The downfall of Henry Courtenay, who had been the head of the most important family in Devon, had left a power vacuum. Lord John Russell, who replaced him, had not had sufficient time to build up a power base in the region and gain the loyalty that the Courtenays had possessed.

The impact of Peter Carew

Sir Peter Carew was sent to meet the rebels. He was a Protestant sympathiser and his actions inflamed the situation; he was later reprimanded by the government. The absence of a powerful local family had allowed the unrest to develop and become a regional revolt.

Government forces and attitudes

The setting fire to the barns at Crediton by government forces only added to the tension. Comments about the rebels' attitude and behaviour by members of the gentry caused antagonism. One described the rebels as 'refuse, scum of the whole county'. The rebels exploited these feelings and, according to John Hooker, a contemporary writer, 'the common people noised and spread it about that the gentlemen were altogether bent to overrun, spoil and destroy them', which brought in even more support for the rebels.

The rebel army

The size of the rebel force grew and reached 5000. They did not launch an attack on Exeter but controlled much of the surrounding area. In advancing towards Exeter they displayed a more peaceful element, marching under the banner of the **Five Wounds of Christ**, as had the peaceful Pilgrimage of Grace.

Therefore, although the rebels, from the tone of their demands to the treatment of the gentry, were often aggressive, the behaviour of many of the gentry during and in the years leading up to the unrest had provoked resistance. This was made easier by the absence of a resident member of the nobility who could have stopped the unrest at the outset.

How far do you agree?

Read Passage A, then use your own knowledge to agree with, or to challenge the argument.

Argument in passage	Knowledge to corroborate the argument	Knowledge to challenge the argument

PASSAGE A

Adapted from John Guy, Tudor England *(1990)*

The 1549 revolts were the closest thing Tudor England saw to a class war. After the Devon and Cornish rebels united, they refused to treat with any gentleman accompanied by his servants on the grounds that 'serving man trusts gentleman'. Although this shows that the people were divided it confirms that the rebels distrusted the gentry. When the rebels besieged Exeter, they lacked recognised gentry leadership. Also their demand that half of the former monastic lands be restored implies that persons who had acquired the land were not involved. But the leaders came from just outside the governing class: Arundell was a 'mere' gentleman; Underhill and Segar were from yeoman backgrounds; and Maunder was a tradesman.

Using knowledge to support or contradict

Read Passage B below. Summarise the interpretation about the violence of the Western Rebels and then develop a counter-argument:

Interpretation offered by the passage:

_____

_____

Counter-argument:

_____

_____

PASSAGE B

Adapted from Barrett L. Beer, Rebellion and Riot *(1982)*

The behaviour of the rebels leaves little doubt that the gentry were the principal adversaries, for the commons expressed anger and resentment towards the ruling elite throughout Devon and Cornwall. While the formal demands of the rebels touched on the social question only in regard to limiting the household servants of the gentry and restoring church lands, the rebels' actions are a better guide to their disposition. From the beginning to the end the Western Rebellion found the commons fighting on one side and the leading gentry on the other.

Political stability and the impact of the Western Rebellion REVISED

It could be argued that the Western Rebellion was the most serious threat of all Tudor rebellions to the government.

- It presented a direct challenge to the government's religious policies.
- It occurred at a time when the government was particularly weak.
- The rebels forced the government into a series of battles.
- It took a significant amount of time for it to be crushed.

However, if one argues that the rebellion was motivated more by social and economic concerns then it appears to be less of a threat.

The rebellion as a threat to the government

- The rebellion took place during a royal minority, which allowed many to argue that Somerset did not have the right to change religion.
- The government also faced a series of riots and rebellions throughout south, east and central England as well as war with Scotland and the threat of invasion from France.
- Because of these other challenges, the government was slow to send troops to the west, allowing the rebellion to develop.
- Moreover, the government's knowledge about the rebellion meant they were slow to realise just how serious it was.
- The rebels themselves were able to force government forces into battle, despite not being well armed.
- The authorities in Exeter were certainly concerned about the threat presented and took measures to prevent the city falling (see page 82); the numbers put to death after the rebellion also suggests that the government saw it as a threat. This is perhaps reinforced by the lack of support for the government's religious policy, with a leading official, William Paget, commenting that the new religion had not won the support of people.

The rebellion was not a threat

Although it raised 5000 men, the size of the force and its failure to link up with other rebel groups meant that it was less of a threat than the Pilgrimage of Grace which had raised 40,000. The government was eventually able to raise a force to defeat it. The rebels did not want to overthrow the dynasty or government and if the aims were more economic and social than religious then it was even less of a threat. The rebels not only failed to take Exeter, but did not leave the south-west to threaten London. It could also be argued (see page 82) that it was government actions that made the situation worse.

Regional instability

Some historians have argued that the rising was due to recent instability in the south-west following the fall of the Courtenays, which created a power vacuum. The government was aware of its weak position and had established the Council of the West in 1539, but this was kept in place for just two years. Russell had not built up a following in the area, and gentry, such as Carew, only added to the difficulties by their aggressive behaviour. Local leaders, such as the Mayor of Bodmin, joined the rebels instead of suppressing them and this was similar to the behaviour of other lesser gentry and members of the civic elite, which further weakened the government position.

The West Country had a tradition of unrest, with the Cornish rising in 1497. Cornwall was cut off from the rest of the country, strongly provincial and resented government interference. There had already been minor incidents of unrest in defence of traditional religion in 1537 at St Keverne and again at Helston in 1548.

Many of the rebels were loyal to the regime and some historians have argued that popular culture used protest to voice objections to unpopular policies, such as religious change. If this is the case, it was government action that turned a peaceful protest into violence.

It might therefore be argued that it was the nature of the West Country and not the recent instability that led to the unrest.

Quick quizzes at **www.hoddereducation.co.uk/myrevisionnotes**

Interpretations: Content or argument?

Read the following interpretation and the two alternative answers to the question. Which answer focuses more on the content and which one focuses more on the arguments in the interpretation? Explain your choice.

> Evaluate the interpretation in the passage and explain how convincing you think it is as an explanation of the seriousness of the Western Rebellion.

Answer 1:

This interpretation argues that the Western Rebellion was not serious. It puts forward the view that it took a long time to suppress only because the government faced a number of challenges to its authority in the south, east and midlands in the summer of 1549 and had to deal with them as well. The interpretation suggests that it was because of these other disturbances that Russell took a long time to reach Exeter and relieve the siege of the city.

Answer 2:

The interpretation puts forward the view that the Western Rebellion was not a serious threat to the government. There is some validity in this view as it did not aim to overthrow the Tudors and if the rebellion was driven by social and economic grievances, as some historians have argued, it was scarcely a major threat to government policy. However, the interpretation is correct to argue that the main reason it took so long to put down was because of other unrest as Grey, who was to help Russell, had to deal with disturbances in both Oxfordshire and Buckinghamshire before he could join forces. Similarly, government forces were further limited because of war in Scotland and the threat of invasion from France, which gives further credence to the argument that the rebellion lasted so long only because of other problems.

PASSAGE

Adapted from A. Fletcher and D. MacCulloch, Tudor Rebellions *(2008)*

The rebellion never had a real chance of forcing the government to make concessions in its religious policy, and its suppression was only so prolonged because the Western rising coincided with the various 'rebellions of commonwealth' to the east and north. At another time forces could have reached Exeter much more quickly and the rebellion might not have achieved the proportions or significance it did. Russell certainly faced a difficult task when he was sent west in June 1549, though there remain differences of view about how his performance there should be assessed.

Recommended reading

Below is a list of suggested further reading on the Western Rebellion.

- Barrett L. Beer, *Rebellion and Riot*, Kent State University Press (1982), Chapter 3
- M.L. Bush, *The Government Policy of Protector Somerset*, Arnold (1975)
- P. Caraman, *The Western Rising*, Westcountry Books (1999)
- A. Fletcher and D. MacCulloch, *Tudor Rebellions*, Longman (2008), Chapter 5
- Nicholas Fellows, *Disorder and Rebellion in Tudor England*, Hodder (2001)
- J. Loach, *Edward VI*, Yale (1999)
- R. Whiting, *The Blind Devotion of the English People*, CUP (1989)
- A. Wood, *The 1549 Rebellions and the Making of Early Modern England*, CUP (2007)

Exam focus

Below is a sample high-level essay in response to an exam-style question on the Western Rebellion. Read the essay and the comments around the answer.

Evaluate the interpretations in both of the passages and explain which you think is more convincing as an explanation of the threat posed by the Western Rebellion.

PASSAGE A

Adapted from Barrett L. Beer, Rebellion and Riot *(1982)*

The gentry and local officials could not manage affairs in the west, intervention by the government was imperative. Somerset might have been more successful if the Western Rebellion had been an isolated event, but beginning in the spring of 1549, he faced a series of worsening crises which weakened his authority. Although Somerset was warned to proceed more cautiously, the rush of events overwhelmed the government and forced it to react defensively.

Preachers were sent to the west to proclaim the reformed Gospel, whilst Somerset waited for the gentry to restore order. Later Somerset dispatched the Carews to help the gentry resist the rebel force. Offenders were to be pardoned. Those who refused pardon were to be apprehended. The Carews could not implement Somerset's policy; and when Sir Peter returned to London he was greeted with indignation.

The Councillors assumed that the rebels could be duped easily and induced to abandon their leaders. These hopelessly erroneous assumptions were made at a time when the rebel army, vastly larger than the government force, was laying siege to Exeter. The government's inept directive may have resulted from Somerset's leniency toward the rebels but was more likely the result of misinformation and poor communication.

PASSAGE B

Adapted from Nicholas Fellows and Mary Dicken, England 1485–1603 *(2015)*

Somerset faced more determined and widespread opposition than any other Tudor government. The harmony of Tudor society collapsed and class hostility flared up. The rebellion had the potential to cause serious problems for the government and if there had been co-ordination between the regions government resources may have been overwhelmed. However, the aims of the rebels were not to overthrow the government, but to bring about changes to government policy. The rebels did not advance on the capital, unlike either the Peasants' Revolt of 1381 or Jack Cade in 1450. Although the number of rebels was quite large, they were no match for government forces, particularly the mercenaries. Some 3000 rebels were killed in battle and further retribution followed, with executions without trials and the confiscation of property. When the government was forced into military action and had sufficient forces it dealt with the rebels quickly and efficiently, without heavy losses of capital or men.

Although both passages put forward the view that the rebellion had the potential to be serious, Passage A does argue that it was a more serious threat than B. A regards it as a threat, in part because of the context, but also because of the government's response. On the other hand, whilst B does acknowledge the seriousness of the rising because of the wider problems in Tudor society, it also argues that it was less of a threat as it did not intend to overthrow the government and, once the government had enough forces, was easily defeated.

Passage A is correct to argue that those involved in government were unable to 'manage affairs' as following the fall of the Courtenays in 1538 there was no one with sufficient influence to control the area. As a result, many of the gentry, instead of trying to put down the rising fled, some to St Michael's Mount. Moreover, it is valid to argue Somerset faced a growing crisis as rebellion broke out in twenty-six counties across most of south and central England, whilst there was also a threat of invasion from France. The passage is also correct

> The views of the two passages are clearly outlined and both the similarities and differences are acknowledged.

to argue that the information the government received was out of date as the initial rising had become large scale before the government was aware and the sending of Carew only made matters worse because of his Protestant views. Therefore, as Passage A argues, the rebellion certainly appeared to be a threat to the government, but this view ignores its limited aims and the ability of the government to respond once it had full details.

In light of Passage A covering only the outbreak of unrest, Passage B is more valid in its view of the threat posed by the rebellion as it deals with the whole period of the rebellion. It is true that Somerset faced more widespread opposition than any other Tudor government, as the widespread risings of the summer of 1549 show, but it is also correct to argue that, despite this, the nature of the aims limited the threat. None of the rebellions aimed at overthrowing the state and most were driven by economic hardship or social grievances. It also correctly argues that the rebels did not threaten London, with the Western rebels laying siege to Exeter. Moreover, as the passage suggests, the rising was crushed with relative ease, although it does not mention that it took five skirmishes or battles. However, the crushing victory at Sampford Courtenay does support the view that it was not a serious threat.

Both passages correctly acknowledge that the rebellion had at least the potential to be a serious threat to the government. However, ultimately they differ in the seriousness of that threat, with Passage A viewing the rebellion as a greater threat than Passage B. Although Passage A is correct to see the threat it caused because of the context of the rebellion, such as war with France and Scotland and the government handling of it, unlike Passage B it does not consider the ease with which the rebels were defeated at Fenny Bridges and Sampford Courtenay once the government had assembled a large enough force. Passage B, whilst acknowledging the potential threat to the government, balances that against the rebels' aims, their movements, and the ultimate outcome to show that the government's position was not threatened, as the rebels did not aim to overthrow the government. It is therefore more convincing as an interpretation.

The margin notes:

Own knowledge is applied to Passage A to evaluate the view. The knowledge is quite detailed and relevant to the actual question. The paragraph considers both the strength and weaknesses of the view offered.

As with the previous paragraph, knowledge is used to evaluate the view offered. Once again the response does consider both the strength and weakness of the view offered.

A supported judgement is reached as to which view is more valid. The response acknowledges that both passages have validity in their views, but explains clearly why B is stronger.

The response explains the views of the two passages, and whilst seeing that both suggest the rebellion had the potential to be serious, it also explains the differences. Own knowledge is used to evaluate the two passages and this is clearly linked to them rather than simply being deployed. The conclusion is particularly strong as not only is the judgement supported, but it also acknowledges that even Passage A has its strengths.

Exam focus activity

When evaluating the passages, it is important that the knowledge is directly linked to the actual passages. Identify where in the response this is done. There is also other knowledge that could have been applied to both passages. Choose one of the passages and write an evaluative paragraph using other knowledge.

7 Depth study: Tyrone's rebellion

The causes of Tyrone's rebellion

There was more unrest in Ireland under Elizabeth I than under any other Tudor monarch. Tyrone's rebellion, which broke out in 1594, lasted longer than any other rebellion. It had a number of possible causes:

● Increased English interference in Ireland.
● The religious policies and **plantation system** pursued by the government.

However, some have argued that it was the government's policy of neglect that prompted the rising, whilst others have seen it as the first nationalist unrest, appealing as the rebellion did to a larger range of people than was usually the case with Irish risings.

The plantation system and religion

In Connaught and Munster land had been confiscated from rebels and granted to English and local landlords at reduced prices. This system, known as plantation, not only resulted in the new landowners increasing rents, but led to an increase in the number of Protestants coming into the area. As a result, more Protestant churches were built and this may have given the rising a religious dimension.

The clan system

The introduction of new landowners was seen by many Irish chieftains as an attack on the traditional Irish system. They saw their position in Irish society and their power under attack and therefore they lost trust in the English **Deputies** who ruled Ireland for the queen. The government needed their support to retain control and establish some form of law and order.

It was certainly true that **Hugh O'Neill**, Earl of Tyrone, who had come to power in **Ulster** considered that his position was under threat. He had originally aided the English garrisons, but in the 1590s he changed sides as he did not feel that his contribution to government was sufficiently recognised. He therefore made contact with Spain.

The policy of neglect

Although the plantation system suggests that the English government was attempting to increase both its influence and control over Ireland, some have argued that Elizabeth followed a policy of neglect and that this led to unrest. This interpretation argues that due to the financial pressures of war against Spain, and funding Dutch rebels, expenditure on Ireland was low. Elizabeth's Deputy in Ireland, Fitzwilliam, was old and he failed to keep order, resulting in increasing factional disputes in Dublin. This allowed **clan** warfare to develop, which saw cattle-raiding and summary executions.

These developments created a problem for Elizabeth as she needed to secure Ireland and prevent the Spanish from taking it and using it as a base from which to invade England.

However, Elizabeth's policies or her neglect, depending on your view, allowed Tyrone to raise the country against her rule. His aim was obviously to increase his own power and influence, but also to drive the English out and, some have argued, achieve independence.

Interpretation: Content or argument?

Read the following interpretation and the two alternative answers to the question. Which answer focuses more on the content and which focuses more on the arguments in the interpretation? Explain your choice.

> Evaluate the interpretations in both of the two passages and explain which you think is the more convincing explanation of the reasons for the outbreak of Tyrone's rebellion.

Answer 1:

The interpretation is arguing that Tyrone's ambition to rule Ulster without interference from English officials was what drove him into rebellion. The interpretation argues that he realised that he now lacked influence in England and that Ireland was being run by minor English officials and adventurers. He was keen to be named 'The O'Neill' and he saw all these things getting in his way and therefore abandoned his position as an Anglo-Irish noble to pursue his personal ambition.

Answer 2:

The interpretation is correct to argue that O'Neill was ambitious and felt that his position and status in Ireland was being undermined by the appointment of minor English officials and adventurers. This had been made clear when he failed to secure a commission from Elizabeth to govern Ulster. The interpretation is correct that he abandoned his position as an Anglo-Irish noble as he turned to get support from Gaelic Ireland, where traditional antagonism to the English meant many were willing to support him and he was able to build up a large fighting force. The interpretation is also correct to argue that he wanted to gain the Gaelic title, 'The O'Neill' and this occurred in 1593. Therefore the interpretation is correct to argue that O'Neill was ambitious and that he wanted power over Ulster.

THE CAUSES OF THE TYRONE REBELLION

Adapted from John Warren, Elizabeth I: Religion and Foreign Affairs *(2002)*

After the death of Shane O'Neill, the government had adopted a cautious approach in Ulster. Attempts were made to play one chieftain off against the other to prevent the rise of another dominant lord. Hugh O'Neill was educated as a royal ward and attached to Leicester's household. He was in time granted the title Earl of Tyrone and was an obvious candidate for the Gaelic title of 'The O'Neill' which was an attractive prospect to him. He also liked being an Anglo-Irish noble. However, as time went on, it became clear to him that he lacked influence where it mattered most in Elizabethan England. His friends there were dead and he had no one to speak for him. He saw Ireland increasingly at the mercy of relatively minor English officials and adventurers: the title Earl of Tyrone would not alone enable him to fulfil his ambition of ruling Ulster without interference.

 Summarise the arguments

Below is a sample exam question and above is a passage referred to in the question. You must read the passage and identify the interpretation offered. Look for the arguments in the interpretation.

> Evaluate the interpretations in both of the two passages and explain which you think is the more convincing explanation of the impact of Tyrone's ambition on the outbreak of unrest in Ireland in 1595.

Interpretation offered by the passage:

_____

_____

The nature of Tyrone's rebellion

Tyrone's rebellion was a serious problem for Elizabeth. Irish rebellions tended to last longer than English rebellions and Tyrone's was no exception. It was the longest lasting of all Tudor rebellions and ended only after Elizabeth's death.

Why was the rebellion serious?

- The rebellion coincided with threats from Spain and further **Armadas** being sent by Philip II. It was a constant concern that the Irish rebels would allow Spanish troops to land and use Ireland as a base from which to attack England. These fears were confirmed in 1601 when Spanish forces landed at Kinsale to join up with Tyrone.
- The problem was made worse for Elizabeth by her financial problems, which meant she lacked the resources to send to Ireland to suppress the unrest.
- Tyrone had been able to capture a key fort on the River Blackwater, which guarded one of the main entries to Ulster.
- He was also able to defeat the English at Yellow Ford in 1598, which allowed him to seize Munster and therefore control much of Ireland. It was very rare for English forces to be defeated by rebels and this added to Elizabeth's concerns.

However, how far the success of the rebellion was due to the strength of Tyrone and how much it was due to Elizabeth's response is a matter for debate.

Tyrone's strengths

- Tyrone had been able to raise the largest rebel force assembled, gaining support from across the country. In the past most unrest had been confined to particular provinces and was confined to one clan, but this rebellion had the characteristics of a national rising.
- His control of Ulster meant that he had a good supply of resources. His forces were well trained as many had experience of serving in Elizabeth's armies and were therefore battle-hardened. He was also able to call on **mercenaries** and reinforcements from Scotland, so his force was not typical of many rebel armies.
- Tyrone himself was a competent leader and well trained in ambush.
- His knowledge of the Irish countryside allowed him to conduct a guerrilla campaign.

Government mistakes

Government resources were stretched because of the financial demands caused by the war with Spain, but it did mean that expenditure on Ireland was low. As a result, many in Ireland felt alienated and had little reason to show loyalty to the government. In England, Elizabeth's council was divided over its approach to Ireland. Elizabeth wanted to adopt a peaceful policy, whilst many councillors argued that she needed to be more aggressive.

The Earl of Essex was sent to Ireland as **Lord Deputy**, but this was a mistake. He was ill-suited to the task and wasted time and money, with troops taking part in endless manoeuvres. He did not give battle to Tyrone, having taken only 4000 men with him. Instead he agreed to a truce and returned to London unauthorised.

He was replaced by Charles Blount, Lord Mountjoy, who was given a large contingent of soldiers. He defeated the Spanish forces that had landed. His three-pronged attack from Armagh, Lough Foyle and Tyrconnel then led to Tyrone's defeat and surrender.

The speed with which he had defeated Tyrone suggests that it was government mistakes that were mainly responsible for the longevity of the rebellion. His army was only the same size as Essex's, but his policy was much more forceful.

How far do you agree?

Read the following passage, then use your own knowledge to agree with, or to challenge the argument.

Argument in passage	Knowledge to corroborate the argument	Knowledge to challenge the argument

PASSAGE

The seriousness of Tyrone's rebellion. Adapted from Nicholas Fellows and Mary Dicken, England 1485–1603, Hodder (2016)

The rebellion in Ireland led by the O'Neill chieftain, the Earl of Tyrone, was a serious matter. In 1598 Tyrone captured a key fort on the River Blackwater, guarding one of the main entries to Ulster. He defeated and killed the English commander at Yellow Ford in 1598 and only half the English troops returned safely to their base in Armagh. He was now able to seize Munster and drive out the English settlers and take control of most of Ireland. This was a real threat and prevented further action against Spain from being contemplated. This was easily the greatest threat to the Tudors in Ireland and was only overcome by heavy expenditure and the talents of Mountjoy.

Support your judgement

Read the sample exam question and two basic judgements below. Support the judgement that you agree with more strongly by adding a reason and evidence that justifies the judgement.

> Evaluate the interpretations in both of the two passages and explain which you think is the more convincing explanation of the seriousness of Tyrone's rebellion.

Answer 1:

Tyrone's rebellion was a serious threat to the English government only because of the policies that the English pursued.

Answer 2:

Tyrone's rebellion was a serious threat to the English government, not only because it was the first national rising, but it was also able to gain foreign support from Spain.

Tip: Whichever option you choose you will have to weigh up both sides of the argument. You could use words such as 'whereas' and 'although' in order to help the process of evaluation.

The impact and threat of Tyrone's rebellion

Rebellions in Ireland have sometimes been seen as less of a threat to English governments because they were so far away. However, they were the most costly to put down and usually required a larger force. They also offered the potential to foreign powers of a landing place from which an invasion of England could be launched and this was the case with Tyrone's.

Ireland was becoming an increasing threat to stability and therefore had a profound impact on the government. Much of this threat was the result of England's changing relations with Ireland since 1534 and it is important to understand the impact of those changes. However, historians have disagreed over whether the threat was due to changes in Ireland or the policy of the English government.

Changes in Ireland

- Ireland was an unruly country where feuding was an everyday feature of life.
- The country was only partly under English control, with English law and government largely confined, in practice, to the area round Dublin known as the **Pale**.
- The structure of the population and its culture and religion of the country only added to the problems. The population was a mixture of Gaelic and Anglo-Norman cultures; whilst the Gaelic and Old English families remained staunchly Catholic, the new settlers were often Protestant and therefore this created a religious divide.
- Catholicism had not only survived, but continued to grow because of **missionaries**. This increased the dislike for Protestantism, which was associated with English rule. This was further reinforced by intervention from both the **papacy** and Spain.

English influence was therefore limited. The great Irish earldoms would have to be crushed if the English were to increase their influence. Gaelic society was very different in terms of land ownership and property rights and now religious differences only added to the gulf.

English government policy

English government intervention had been increasing since 1534 and, rather than increasing stability, attempts at centralisation had caused instability. Government policy was confused and not consistent. Not only did the English not understand Gaelic customs and traditions, but attempts to impose their own only added to resentment, seen most clearly with the attempts to enforce Protestantism. This decision resulted in the replacement of papal authority with that of the monarch.

However, attempts to impose greater control was attempted at the same time as expenditure was reduced. The government also introduced the **plantation system**, which as well being run on the cheap was also not given time to succeed.

Appointments only added to the instability. Elizabeth appointed unsuitable men to serve as Lord Deputy, such as Essex and Grey, and it was not until **Mountjoy** was sent that the government finally supported the reforms of able **Deputies**, such as Sidney.

As a result, the nature of Irish society and English government policy made the situation worse. The Irish resented English interference and had lost trust in the whole system, undermining what limited stability there had been.

How far do you agree?

Read the following passage, then use your own knowledge to agree with, or to challenge the argument.

Argument in passage	Knowledge to corroborate the argument	Knowledge to challenge the argument

PASSAGE

The impact of Tyrone's rebellion on the English government. Adapted from John Warren, Elizabeth I: Religion and Foreign Affairs (2002)

By 1595, Tyrone was in open rebellion and looking for help from Spain. Philip II was not one to throw away money on lost causes, but Tyrone's effective and modernised army interested him, especially when it became clear that Elizabeth's forces were finding it a formidable opponent. The success of Tyrone revealed the folly of Elizabeth's past meanness. All the penny-pinching, free-enterprise schemes, all the inadequate but still substantial monies provided for the campaigns of the Lord Deputies, all the attempts to 'civilise' the Gaelic Irish, all in jeopardy and all potentially wasted. Indeed if Tyrone were to succeed in linking up with a Spanish invasion force then the English might well be forced back into the Pale and the surrounding southern counties. It was, indeed, a close run thing.

Support your judgement

Read the following sample exam question and two basic judgements. Support the judgement that you agree with more strongly by adding a reason and evidence that justifies the judgement.

> Evaluate the interpretations in both of the two passages and explain which you think is the more convincing explanation of the threat to stability presented by Tyrone's rebellion.

Answer 1:

Tyrone's rebellion was the culmination of a growing threat posed by Ireland to Tudor governments since 1534. The increasing alienation brought about by a cultural and religious divide created an intractable problem of government.

Answer 2:

To argue that Tyrone's rebellion presented a threat to the stability of England would be a mistake. It was only English government policy that had created instability and once Mountjoy was appointed and reforms of able Deputies were supported then the problem became less serious.

Tip: Whichever option you choose you will have to weigh up both sides of the argument. You could use words such as 'whereas' and 'although' in order to help the process of evaluation.

The interpretation topics

The specification identifies the three topics from which the interpretations question will be drawn. They are:

- the Pilgrimage of Grace
- the Western Rebellion
- Tyrone's rebellion.

In answering this question, you have to assess and evaluate the arguments in the passages by applying your own knowledge of the events to reach a supported judgement as to which is the stronger or more convincing interpretation. This section will give you guidance on how to approach the question and will refer to the two answers in the book to illustrate the points that are being made.

How should the question be approached?

It is probably best to think of a four-paragraph structure to your answer:

- In the first paragraph, explain the interpretations in the two passages – what their view about the issue in the question is – and place them in the wider debate about the issue in the question.
- In the second paragraph, apply your own knowledge to Passage A, so for example with the Exam focus at the end of Section 5 (pages 80–81), apply your knowledge of the causes of the Pilgrimage of Grace to judge how valid the view offered by Passage A is. What do you know about the causes of the Pilgrimage of Grace? Was it due to court faction, were there economic and social causes or was it simply religious? This will allow you to evaluate the validity of the view about the causes of the Pilgrimage of Grace.
- Repeat the second point, but for Passage B: what knowledge do you have about religion as a cause of the Pilgrimage of Grace? How far does it support or challenge the view offered in Passage B about the causes of the Pilgrimage?
- In the final paragraph you need to reach a balanced and supported judgement as to which passage you think is more convincing as evidence for the causes of the Pilgrimage of Grace.

How to evaluate a passage

A good paragraph will do the following:

- Remain focused on the actual wording of the question and not write generally about the topic.
- Directly link the knowledge that you have to the actual interpretation in the passage. Many responses contain a great deal of knowledge, but it is not directly linked to the actual passage and therefore it is not 'used' to evaluate the view in the passage.
- The knowledge is used to explain whether the view of the passage is either valid or invalid.
- It is therefore helpful to build up a list of evaluative words which you can use in your answer; this might include words such as 'however', 'although', 'indeed' and 'moreover'.
- You must use relevant and accurate knowledge to evaluate the view. The depth of knowledge required is no more than what can be found in a standard A Level textbook, such as the Hodder Access book on *Rebellion and Disorder under the Tudors 1485–1603*. The knowledge that is used in the second answer includes reference to the siege of Exeter and the crushing of rebel forces at Sampford Courtenay, as well as the context in which the unrest occurred, all of which are in the textbook.
- You should consider a range of issues raised by the passage and consider both the strengths and limitations of the issues it raises. It is very unlikely that the passage will contain only strengths or only weaknesses, as can be seen in the response to the question on pages 88–89, although overall you might consider that the view it offers about the issue in the question is either strong or limited.

Reaching a judgement

In paragraphs two and three you will have evaluated the views of the two passages. However, in order to reach the higher mark bands you must reach a supported judgement as to which passage's view about the issue in the question you think is more convincing.

A good conclusion will do the following:

- Reach a clear judgement as to which passage's view about the issue in the question is more convincing.
- Explain why a particular passage is more convincing and why the other is less convincing.
- It is likely to suggest that there are some parts in both passages which are more or less convincing. This can be clearly seen in the sample essay (page 89), where the conclusion notes that although A is correct to see the initial threat of the rising, it considers only the outbreak of the unrest and is therefore limited in its view.
- The answer may also note that both passages have their limitations as they do not consider issues which are important; however, be careful not to spend all your time writing about what is missing from the passages – you should focus on what is actually there.
- Provide some support, briefly, for the judgement so that it is not simply assertion. This is done in the sample essay (page 89) through reference to the defeat of the rebels at Fenny Bridges and Sampford Courtenay.

Exam focus activity

Using the two exemplar answers and the information in this section, make a summary of the key points needed in order to produce a high-level answer. Use this as a checklist for any practice papers that you do.

Glossary

Act of Attainder An Act passed by parliament against traitors that took away their land and their family's land.

Alms Money, food or other donations given as charity to the poor.

Anti-enclosure legislation Laws designed to prevent the enclosure of common land.

Arable The growing of crops, such as corn or wheat.

Aragonese Supporters of Henry VIII's queen, Catherine of Aragon. After the divorce and her death, a group of her followers put pressure on Henry to ensure her daughter, Mary Tudor, was restored to the succession.

Armada The naval invasion force sent by Philip II of Spain to invade England in 1588,

Articles A list of grievances drawn up by rebels.

Bailiffs The agent of a landlord, responsible for the running of an estate.

Bigod's rising This rising in 1537 was the final part of the Pilgrimage of Grace. The numbers who rose believing Henry would not keep his promises were much smaller than in 1536 and it allowed Henry to crush it and ignore his earlier promises.

Bonds and recognisances Bonds bound people to the crown to undertake a certain action or pay money. A recognisance was the acknowledgement to fulfil the commitment.

Castleward A former military service which required tenants to defend Norwich Castle; it was replaced by the payment of rent.

Catholic recusants Catholics who did not attend their local parish churches. At the start of the Elizabethan period many had attended, but with the influence of missionary priests many were encouraged to stay away.

Cecil faction The supporters of William, and later Robert, Cecil.

Chamberlain The manager of the monarch's household.

Chantries Chapels where prayers for the dead were said to reduce their time in purgatory.

Churchwardens Officers responsible for the financial arrangements of their parish churches.

Clan A group of people of common descent, or a group of families.

'Class war' A conflict between different classes in a community with different social or economic positions.

Common land Grazing land in a village that was available for everyone, even if they owned no land. It would not be fenced.

Commoners A common person without rank or high status.

Constables The governor of a royal castle.

Council of the North Established by Richard III to run the area north of the Trent, it was based in York. It was reformed after both the Pilgrimage of Grace and the rising of the Northern Earls.

County levies A local body of troops raised in a county.

Coup The illegal seizure of power, usually by force.

Debased the coinage The reduction of the gold and silver content of the coinage, although the value of the coins remained the same. It helped to cause inflation as people did not trust the new coinage and so prices rose.

Decaying towns In the sixteenth century many towns were in economic decline and suffered from the problems of high unemployment and poverty.

Deputy Lieutenants They assisted Lord Lieutenants in the running of the county. They usually came from the leading gentry.

Devise The document by which Edward VI attempted to deprive Mary of the throne and replace her with Lady Jane Grey.

Divine Right of Kings The concept that the right to rule comes to kings from God.

Elizabethan Church Settlement This usually refers to the Acts of Uniformity and Supremacy, passed at the start of Elizabeth I's reign, which established a moderate form of Protestantism. It established the organisation, ritual and teaching of the Church.

Enclosure Commission Established by Protector Somerset in 1548 to look into enclosures and determine their legality. Its establishment encouraged many commoners that Somerset was on their side and led to them pulling down fences and resulted in many riots.

Enclosures The hedging, often of land with common grazing rights, by a landlord so that they can graze large flocks of sheep.

English Bibles A number of Bibles were produced in English, but the first official version was the Great Bible in 1540; this replaced the Latin Bible, making it more available to those who could read.

Entry fines A fee paid by a tenant to renew their lease or by a new tenant following the death of the previous tenant.

Excommunication The formal exclusion of someone from the Church, condemning them to eternal damnation.

Exeter Conspiracy In 1538 the government claimed to have uncovered a plot. Named after the Marquis of Exeter, Henry Courtenay. He was supposed to have conspired with his brothers to overthrow Henry VIII and restore Catholicism. It resulted in the execution of the Marquis, Lord Montague and the elderly Countess of Salisbury.

Faction A group of people with similar views who joined together in order to gain influence and remove those who were influencing the monarch.

Five Wounds of Christ A banner that displayed the five wounds of Christ following his crucifixion.

Fixed rate An agreed rate that could not be changed.

Folding cattle Allowing cattle and sheep to graze on land after the harvest in order to manure it.

Food riots Shortages of grain in the 1580s and 1590s resulted in food riots in the south of England, notably Somerset, Kent, Sussex, Gloucestershire and Hampshire.

Forced loans A tax raised without the approval of parliament.

Garrisoning policy The placing of soldiers in a town to protect it.

Gentry The class below the nobility. They were usually men of some wealth and land holding from well-bred families.

Grants of monopolies Under Elizabeth I rights were given to courtiers to be the sole manufacturer or trader in a certain article. This allowed them to set their own prices.

Great Chain of Being A strict hierarchical structure for everything in the universe, set out by God.

Great Council Meetings of the great men of the kingdom, called to give the monarch advice. Used frequently by Henry VII.

Guerrilla warfare Irregular fighting, usually avoiding open warfare and conducted by smaller forces against larger ones.

Heretics People who departed from the established beliefs of the Catholic Church, the usual punishment was burning.

High politics Politics that affected the ruling classes, such as the succession, rather than low politics, such as enclosure, that affected the lower classes.

Holy Roman Emperor The elected ruler of lands that today include Germany, but their authority was limited and much of the area was ruled by independent princes. In theory they had more power, but in reality this was not the case.

Homilies Official lessons that priests could read to the congregation.

Hosts The name given to the various regional armies that were formed in the north of England during the Pilgrimage of Grace.

Household servants The personal servants and staff of the monarch or noble. The monarch's household servants were part of the court.

Inflation A rise in prices relative to wages so that the purchasing power of wages declines.

Injunctions A series of orders issued by Cromwell to priests. It instructed them about what should be taught and how the churches should be decorated.

Innovative taxation New forms of taxation or taxation that ignored traditional practices, such as the exclusion of the northern counties from paying taxes to fund wars against France as they had to pay for the defence of the northern borders.

Jurisdictional control The power to make legal decisions over certain areas.

Justices of the Peace (JPs) Appointed for every county, they served for a year. They were unpaid and usually local gentry whose job it was to see that laws were obeyed in the county. They gradually replaced sheriffs and during the Tudor period they took on an increasing number of responsibilities.

Knighthood The title, rank or status of a knight.

Lord Deputy Appointed by the monarch and ruled Ireland in their name. They could be English, Irish or Anglo-Norman.

Lord Lieutenants They were appointed by the monarch, with one for each county. Their main task was to organise the county militia.

Lord President of the Council The title taken by the Duke of Northumberland when he replaced the Duke of Somerset as head of the Regency Council.

Lord Protector The title given to the Duke of Somerset when he headed the Regency Council to rule during the minority of Edward VI.

Magistrates An official who runs a legal court that deals with minor offences.

Martial law The replacement of civil rule by military rule.

Mercenaries Overseas professional soldiers who were paid to fight.

Minor The term used to describe a child before they attain majority and are able to act independently.

Missionary priest A priest from overseas sent to help the conversion of a country.

Non-parliamentary tax An imposed tax not levied with parliamentary authority.

Oaths of Succession and Supremacy Oaths given to office holders following Henry VIII's divorce swearing to accept the change in the succession and his right to be Head of the Church.

Oaths of Supremacy and Uniformity Anyone taking public or church office in England had to swear allegiance to the monarch as supreme governor of the Church of England and to accept the newly established set form of worship.

Order of the Garter A prestigious honour awarded by the monarch.

Overseers of the poor Officials whose job it was to administer the Poor Law and distribute relief.

Pageant A public entertainment in the form of a procession or the outdoor performance of an historical scene.

Pale The area around Dublin where English rule was secure.

Papacy The authority or office of the pope.

Papal bull A decree issued by the pope.

Papal sanction The approval of the pope.

Particularism Allegiance to the local area before the country. This declined as the sixteenth century progressed.

Pasture Land used for the grazing of sheep.

Patronage The support given by a patron to an individual or a group.

Peasants' Revolt In 1381 Kent and Essex, under John Ball and Wat Tyler, revolted against new and high levels of taxation to fund war against France.

Peerages The granting of noble status.

Penal laws Laws that were passed in the 1570s that punished non-attendance at Church.

Peripheral The regions on the edge of England, such as the borders with Scotland or the West Country.

Pilgrims' ballad A song written by the protestors during the Pilgrimage of Grace; it criticised many of the king's ministers.

Plantation system In Ireland where land was taken from rebels and granted to English and local landlords at reduced rates.

Poor Law Laws brought in during the sixteenth century to look after the poor following the closure of the monasteries. The laws gradually discriminated between different types of poor, punishing those who could work, but giving aid to those who were unable through illness or age.

Prayer Book Book containing the order of services to be used in the Church. This was changed during the reign of Edward VI and the new Prayer Book issued in 1549 provoked the Western Rebellion.

Pretenders This was a problem for Henry VII. The Yorkists put forward Simnel and Warbeck who claimed to be the Earl of Warwick and the Duke of York respectively. They had stronger claims to the throne than Henry VII.

Privy Council A body of advisors, chosen by the monarch. It was their duty to carry out royal decisions.

Prorogue The ending of a parliamentary session without dissolving parliament. This meant that the parliament could be recalled.

Provincialism Loyalty is firstly to the local area or county rather than the country.

Reformation The religious changes that saw England break away from the Catholic Church and establish a separate, independent church of which the monarch was the head.

Relics Religious artefacts, claimed to be the remains or personal belongings of a saint or other religious figure.

Richard II He was overthrown as King of England in 1390 by Henry Bolingbroke. The performance of the play reminded people that the removal of a monarch had a precedent.

Royal progresses Official journeys made by the monarch around the country, usually in the summer months and confined to the south and central England, staying with nobles and members of the gentry.

Saffron A costly spice with a strong golden yellow colour.

Serfs A term used to describe peasants who are tied to the land on which they work.

Sheep and Cloth tax Taxes on the size of sheep flocks and the production of cloth that Edward VI's government proposed to introduce in 1549.

Sheep-corn areas Areas of mixed farming where both grain was grown and sheep were raised.

Sheriffs The chief officer of the crown in each county.

Six Articles The Act upheld traditional Catholic practices and remained in force until 1547.

Standing army A full-time army. England did not have the finances to pay for one.

Statute of Uses A law which altered the way property could be left in a will.

Steward An officer of the royal household, often responsible for running crown lands.

Stone altars Traditional altars in the Catholic Church were made of stone, but during Edward's reign they were replaced with wooden altars. This was symbolic of the change in the meaning of the eucharist from a sacrifice to an act of remembrance.

Subsidy A parliamentary tax.

Subsidy Act An Act of Parliament agreeing to the levying of a certain amount of money.

The 'sweat' A form of influenza.

Tenants Farmers who did not own the land they farmed, but rented it. They paid a fixed rent for a certain number of years.

Treaty of Ayton Treaty with Scotland in 1497. Scotland ended their support for Warbeck.

Treaty of Étaples Treaty with France, signed in 1492, by which the French agreed not to give support to Yorkist pretenders and also pay a pension to the English king.

Ulster A province in the north of Ireland.

Usurper A person who seizes power illegally.

Visitations Like an inspection when the visitors would question either monks or clergy about the religious conditions.

Wage labourers Workers who rely solely on wages for their income, they have no land to farm and earn an income.

Warrant A document allowing the arrest, search or seizure of goods.

Writ A legal command ordering a person to act or behave in a certain way.

Yeomen These were farmers below the rank of gentry, but owned their own land and made a substantial income from it.

Yorkist Supporter of the House of York, one of the two families who had fought in the Wars of the Roses in the fifteenth century against the House of Lancaster. The family had a strong claim to the throne through relatives of the previous monarchs, Edward IV and Richard III.

Key figures

Reginald Bray (c. 1440–1503) He had originally worked for Margaret Beaufort, but became Chancellor of the Duchy of Lancaster under Henry VII and was his chief financial and property administrator.

Catherine of Aragon (1485–1536) The first wife of Henry VIII, she had previously been married to Henry's elder brother, Arthur. She was the mother of Mary, but bore no surviving sons. The annulment of her marriage to Henry proved to be the catalyst for Henry's break with the Catholic Church.

Thomas Cranmer (1489–1556) Cranmer defended Henry's divorce from Catherine of Aragon and was appointed Archbishop of Canterbury in 1533. He wrote the Prayer Book during Edward VI's reign, but was burned for his beliefs by Mary.

Thomas Cromwell (1485–1540) Henry VIII's chief minister after the fall of Thomas Wolsey until his own fall and execution in 1540. He had been the architect of the break with Rome and the Dissolution of the Monasteries.

Lord Thomas Darcy (c. 1467–1537) Darcy served both Henry VII and Henry VIII. He opposed the Dissolution of the Monasteries and was convicted of treason, along with Lord John Hussey, following his part in the Pilgrimage of Grace. He was executed on Tower Hill in 1537.

Robert Devereux, 2nd Earl of Essex (1567–1601) His father died when he was nine and his mother then married the Earl of Leicester. Essex graduated from Cambridge, became Elizabeth's favourite courtier in the 1580s and was made Master of the Horse and given the monopoly over sweet wins. He married Walsingham's daughter in 1591 and temporarily lost favour. However in 1591 he commanded the royal force that aided Henry of Navarre and was made a Privy Councillor. He helped in the defeat of the Spanish at Cadiz in 1597 and was then sent to Ireland as commander. His performance in Ireland was poor, making a truce with Tyrone and returning to court without permission, bursting into the Queen's bedchamber. He was put under house arrest and dismissed. this led to him organising a rising to try and regain his position. With the failure of the rising he was arrested, tried and executed in 1601.

James Fitzmaurice Fitzgerald (d. 1579) A member of the Geraldine dynasty in Ireland, he resisted the influence of the English Protestants and Elizabeth and led the Desmond Rebellions against her forces.

Thomas FitzGerald (see Silken Thomas).

John Flowerdew A lawyer and landowner who clashed with Robert Kett in 1549 over the enclosure of their respective lands, causing rebels, led by Kett, to riot.

Francis I (1494–1547) King of France from 1515 to 1547. His main rival was the Holy Roman Emperor, but Henry VIII also saw him as a rival and England was in frequent conflict with France, often in alliance with the Emperor.

Lady Jane Grey (1537–54) She was the great-granddaughter of Henry VII and first cousin once removed of Edward VI. Her parents were the Duke of Suffolk and Lady Frances Brandon. She married Guildford Dudley, the son of the Duke of Northumberland and Edward's Lord President of the Council, against her wishes. In June 1553 Edward VI, through the Devise, named her as his heir to prevent the throne passing to his Catholic half-sister, Mary Tudor. Jane was very reluctantly crowned queen, but lasted for only nine days before Mary took the throne. She was imprisoned and charged with treason, but initially her life was spared. However, following Wyatt's rebellion in 1554 she was executed.

Lord John Hussey (1466–1537) He was knighted by Henry VII and served as Chief Butler to Henry VIII. He had close connections with Catherine of Aragon and was Mary's chamberlain and his wife was one of her attendants. Found guilty of treason following the Pilgrimage of Grace in 1536 he was executed for his part in this rebellion.

Robert Kett (1492–1549) He led men from Norfolk in rebellion against the enclosure of common lands, enforced by the Duke of Somerset. The rebellion was quashed and he was executed at Norwich in 1549.

Earl of Kildare (1487–1534) A member of the prominent Fitzgerald family, he was appointed the Lord Deputy of Ireland. He was unable to maintain peace in Ireland and died in 1534.

John Morton (1420–1500) He was made Archbishop of Canterbury by Henry VII in 1486. He was also the Lord Chancellor and advised the king on finance.

Lord Mountjoy (1563–1606) Charles Blount was an English nobleman. He replaced Essex as Lord

Deputy of Ireland and was responsible for the defeat of the Tyrone rebellion under Elizabeth.

Duke of Norfolk (1536–72) Thomas Howard led the English army in Scotland against Mary of Guise. He was imprisoned in 1569 for scheming to marry Mary Queen of Scots, and was eventually tried and executed for treason in 1572 for his part in the Ridolfi plot to put Mary on the English throne.

Sir Edward Poynings (1459–1521) He was a soldier, administrator and diplomat. He had been governor of Calais, but was sent to Ireland, a Yorkist stronghold, as Lord Deputy by Henry VII. He was able to bring the area to order and loyalty to the Tudor regime.

William Shakespeare (1564–1616) He was an actor and public dramatist who also performed at court. He wrote for the commercial theatre and an audience that was drawn from all classes. His range of works was considerable, including histories, comedies and tragedies, many of which were written in the 1590s. Richard II was performed the night before Essex's rebellion and may have been a warning from Essex that monarchs had been overthrown before. His portrayal of Richard III as a hunchback did much to blacken the king's reputation.

Silken Thomas (1513–37) A member of the Kildare clan, who were seen as the natural rulers of the Pale. The arrest and imprisonment of his father resulted in him leading a rebellion in 1534.

Duke of Somerset (1500–52) The Protector of Edward VI who ruled England from Henry VIII's death in 1547 until his fall following the rebellions of 1549. He was restored to the Council, but was executed in 1552.

Earl of Tyrone: Hugh O'Neill, Earl of Tyrone (c. 1540–1616) He had been brought up as a royal ward in Leicester's household, he became Earl of Tyrone in 1584. Although he was an Anglo-Irish noble he felt he did not have enough influence at the English court. And resented the influence of minor English officials. He was dissatisfied with being just Earl and wanted to be chief of the O'Neills. He therefore led the rebellion against English rule and became leader of his clan, the O'Neills. He defeated English forces at Yellow Ford in 1598 before finally being crushed in 1601 at Kinsale. Tyrone left Ireland for Spain in 1605 and died in Rome in 1616.

Perkin Warbeck (1474–99) He became a threat to the Tudor dynasty by claiming to be Richard, Duke of York. He was declared an impostor by Henry VII but made two failed attempts to invade England, the first of these with James IV of Scotland. Once captured by Henry, he was first imprisoned and then executed in 1499.

Thomas Wolsey (1473–1530) Wolsey became a royal councillor in 1510, but rose to prominence through organising the expedition against France in 1513. He became Henry's chief minister and was also made a cardinal. However, he began to lose Henry's trust following the failure of the Amicable Grant, but most significantly when he could not obtain Henry's divorce from Catherine of Aragon.

Thomas Wyatt (1521–54) A soldier who had been involved in the capture of Boulogne under Henry VIII and in the defeat of Northumberland by Mary Tudor. He was MP for Kent, but grew fearful that Mary's marriage to Philip of Spain would result in the loss of patronage for Englishmen. He led a rebellion against Mary in protest at the marriage, was found guilty of high treason and executed in 1554.

Timeline

1485	Battle of Bosworth, Henry VII defeats Richard III ending Yorkist rule
1486	Lovell and Stafford rebellion
1486–87	Simnel rebellion
1487	Statute to limit the number of retainers
1489	Yorkshire tax rebellion, Henry VII re-establishes Council of the North
1497	Cornish tax rebellion. Defeat of Perkin Warbeck
1504	Further statute to limit the number of retainers
1509	Accession of Henry VIII following death of Henry VII
1525	Unrest caused by the Amicable Grant
1529–30	Fall from power and death of Cardinal Thomas Wolsey
1534	Act of Supremacy, Henry VIII made Head of the Church in England
1534–37	Silken Thomas rebellion in Ireland
1536	Reformation Parliament
1536	Closure of the smaller monasteries, Lincolnshire rising and Pilgrimage of Grace
1537	Bigod rising
1538	Injunctions reinforce government attack on saints, pilgrimages and holy days
1539	Act of Six Articles, gives support to more conservative religious practices
1540	Execution of Thomas Cromwell, Henry VIII's chief minister
1543	Act for the Advancement of True Religion limits access to the Bible
1547	Death of Henry VIII, Protector Somerset rules on behalf of Edward VI. Dissolution of the Chantries
1548	Establishment of Enclosure Commission. Unrest at Northaw, Hertfordshire and Helston, Cornwall
1549	Introduction of new Prayer Book, Western and Kett's rebellion, unrest in much of south and central England. Introduction of Lord Lieutenants
1549–50	Overthrow of Duke of Somerset as **Lord Protector** and replaced by Duke of Northumberland
1552	Execution of Duke of Somerset. Rigorous enforcement of anti-enclosure legislation, revalue coinage to halt inflation, arable farming protected and new Poor Law introduced
1553	Death of Edward VI and attempt by Duke of Northumberland to place Lady Jane Grey on the throne fails. Mary Tudor accedes to the throne, Northumberland executed
1554	Wyatt's rebellion. Mary marries Philip of Spain
1558	Death of Mary Tudor, Elizabeth I inherits. Militia Acts
1558–67	Shane O'Neill unrest in Ireland
1559	Elizabethan Church Settlement
1563	Statute of Artificers, Act for the Maintenance of Tillage
1568	Arrival of Mary Queen of Scots in England
1569–70	Plot to marry Mary to Duke of Norfolk, Rebellion of the Northern Earls
1569–73	Munster rebellion
1570	Papal bull excommunicates Elizabeth
1571	Penal laws introduced against Catholic recusants, Ridolfi plot
1572	Council of the North reformed, Poor Law Act
1576	Poor Law Act requires parishes to find work for the able-bodied
1579–83	Geraldine rebellion
1585	Parliament pass Act against Jesuits and seminary priests
1586	Babington Plot, Book of Orders gives advice to JPs on how to deal with food shortages
1587	Execution of Mary Queen of Scots
1588	Defeat of Spanish Armada
1592–93	Statute Regarding the Export of Corn
1595–1603	Tyrone rebellion
1596	Oxfordshire rising
1598	Poor Law Act, Statute against the Conversion to Pasture, Statute against the Engrossing of Farms
1601	Essex rebellion